Island
Buffet

Island Buffet

*Creative Travel
On A Limited Budget*

by YVONNE SCHMITZ

Please scan the QR code to view my
"photo journey" documenting my trip at
www.islandbuffettravel.com

Follow me on Instagram @yvonnes.adventures

Copyright © 2024 Yvonne Schmitz

ISBN: 979-8-9910236-0-3 paperback
ISBN: 979-8-9910236-2-7 ebook

A very special thanks to Wikipedia, Google, ChatGPT, my
drivers, guides, and hosts for the facts about each island. The
information in this book was correct to the best of my knowledge
at the time of publication. The author does not assume liability for
loss or damage caused by errors or omissions.

Some names and identifying details in this book have been
changed to protect the privacy of individuals.

All brand names, trademarks, and registered trademarks
mentioned in this book are the property of their respective
owners. The use of these names, trademarks, and brands is for
identification purposes only and does not imply endorsement
or affiliation. The author has no affiliation with any companies
mentioned; references to specific websites and services are based
on personal preference and experience.

Printed in the United States of America

Cover, Design, and Book Layout by
Connie Roy Reverie Design

Acknowledgments

I would like to thank everyone who helped to bring this book to fruition!

Thank you, Cyndi Pride, Rachel Hayes, and my amazing friend in North Carolina for your eyes and brain in editing. Your investment of time was greatly appreciated!

Thank you, Connie Roy and Reverie Design for creating a beautiful work of art for my cover. Thank you also for formatting and guiding me through the rest of the process of self-editing. You're the BEST!

Thank you, Loren Crundwell, Rob Thompson, Pamela Wimbush-Cady, and Jamie Honden for all your help with ChatGPT, WIX, and Instagram.

Thank you, Marilyn and Larry Shaw for renting my home and giving me this amazing opportunity. I couldn't have asked for better renters!

A huge thanks to my family and friends who faithfully cheered me on by reading and commenting on my daily Facebook posts. You have no idea how much I appreciated the interaction…it was like you were on the adventure with me! Your enthusiasm also encouraged me to find all the cool things to do so I would have something to share with you each day. Hugs for making me feel like I wasn't alone even though I was halfway around the world.

*I'm not rich, but I am creative!
I rented my house out for five months, and used
the rent money to pay for flights and
accommodations to 17 different islands.*

CONTENTS

CONTENTS

CONTENTS

CONTENTS

CONTENTS

CONTENTS

CONTENTS

CONTENTS

Preparing For My Trip

Grabbing the Opportunity

A coworker once told me, "Yvonne, most people talk about doing cool things, but you actually **do** them!" I took this as a huge compliment. I wasn't always brave (just ask my classmates and family), but once I stepped out of my comfort zone as an adult to do strange things or travel to exotic places, I was rewarded with many great experiences. So, when the opportunity of a lifetime came up, I jumped at the chance.

Here's how it all began. One day when I was playing pickleball, two of my Canadian friends told me they were losing their lease on their current rental home and wanted to know if I knew anyone interested in renting out their house. I responded, "Hmmm, what exactly are you looking for?" Over the next few days, we chatted about details, and they came and looked at my house. We negotiated a price and signed a contract. I had absolutely no idea I'd ever rent out my house as a creative way to pay for my travels, but the opportunity fell into my lap that day.

At that exact moment, a quote by Sir Richard Branson popped up on my Facebook page. He said, "If someone offers you an amazing opportunity but you are not sure you can do it, say yes – then learn how to do it later."

So, I was officially going to be homeless for five to six months…now what?

Hmmm, Where Should I Go?

I started by thinking of places on my bucket list…Brazil, Madagascar, Vanuatu, Tahiti, and Bora Bora. I began looking at cruises around the world, but quickly learned they were outside my budget. Additionally, many of the ports of call were duplicates of places I'd already visited. I really wanted to choose islands I'd never been to before.

I shared my plans with my buddy Steve in Australia. He made me realize I needed to check weather patterns. I pulled out a world map and plotted a path, beginning with the islands off the coast of Africa and winding my way through various tropical islands before ending in French Polynesia. I'd never even heard of many of these islands!

I decided to call this trip *Yvonne's Island-Hopping Adventure*.

Crafting the Journey and Budget

Ok, so now that we negotiated a price for the rent on my house, I have my budget for this giant trip away from home. I set aside a percentage of that money to pay taxes on my rental income, then began working with the rest.

Based on previous trip planning experience, I knew airfare had some flexibility based on the sites I normally booked through, Hopper being my personal favorite. It also made a difference with the day booked; for instance, Tuesdays offered tiny savings, and the farther out the flights were booked the better. I began with a tentative outline of flights to all the islands. Once I discovered that I could take the ferry between four of the Society Islands, that reduced the number of flights necessary. As I was exploring airfare, I also discovered that it was cheaper to fly from Seychelles to the Maldives via Sri Lanka. I did a Google search of Sri Lanka and immediately added a seven-day layover there. Also, I added Taiwan and Cook Islands to the list once I saw how close they were. I've always been a traveler who said, "Hey, while you're in the neighborhood..." I took careful notes and watched the airfare on various sites including the airline website itself.

Before I began booking airfare, I started investigating accommodations on all the islands. I took extensive notes and looked for things that were important to me: location, view, A/C, Wi-Fi, washing machine, and access to public transportation since renting a car didn't fit into the budget. My favorite sites were Airbnb, Booking.com, and Expedia.

Once I knew the approximate costs for airfare and what was affordable for accommodation, it was time to start booking! Sadly, that overwater bungalow in Bora Bora wasn't going to happen.

I tried going through travel agencies but found that I could save money by doing it myself. I also rearranged the schedule several times and even added a few islands. Here's the final schedule:

- **Dec 14-18:** Amarillo, TX to visit family for Christmas
- **Dec 20-Jan 1:** Mauritius
- **Jan 1-8:** Réunion
- **Jan 8-22:** Madagascar
- **Jan 22-31:** Seychelles
- **Feb 1-10:** Sri Lanka
- **Feb 10-20:** Maldives
- **Feb 21-28:** Philippines
- **Feb 28-Mar 7:** Taiwan
- **Mar 7-15:** Papua New Guinea
- **Mar 15-22:** Vanuatu
- **Mar 22-30:** New Caledonia
- **Mar 30-Apr 6:** Tonga
- **Apr 6-13:** Cook Islands
- **Apr 13-20:** Tahiti
- **Apr 20-27:** Moorea
- **Apr 27-May 4:** Huahine
- **May 4-12:** Bora Bora
- **May 13:** Tahiti (fly home)
- **May 14:** Ft. Myers, FL

And there you have it, the carefully planned itinerary for my adventure of a lifetime!

4

Travel Entry Essentials: Visas and More

Once the itinerary was set, I started investigating entry requirements for each country. Most countries will allow entry for up to 90 days with a valid passport, which has at least six months before expiration and a couple of blank pages. Some countries will give you a visa upon entry at the airport. Other countries will require a visa, which must be secured before landing.

Papua New Guinea was my toughest one because it asked for many documents. A couple of countries asked for proof of international health coverage. In this case, I requested a letter from my travel insurance company explaining my coverage in case of illness or injury while abroad. I was also asked to show my Covid card to check in for my flight going to Mauritius, so have that and your yellow fever vaccination card with you if traveling to certain African countries. I also had to produce a current bank statement showing that I had sufficient funds to cover my stay while in some countries. Proof of accommodation and an onward flight confirmation were required in a couple of countries as well.

The best way to know what you need is to Google "Entry Requirements" per country, then allow yourself enough time to secure the documents and wait for visa approval. I would suggest keeping a digital and hard copy of visas to show at the airport.

Navigating Flight Fiascos

Because I was working on a tight budget, I did a lot of research before booking each flight between the islands. I found that Hopper, Skyscanner, and Expedia offered some of the best deals. However, because they are a third party, it was sometimes a challenge when the airline made a change and I was notified via Hopper, etc. Most changes were only a few minutes' difference, and I easily adapted to the changes.

My flight from Papua New Guinea to Vanuatu was an entirely different story! I hadn't even left the U.S. when I got an alert from Air Vanuatu that my second leg was changed. This change created a mess because the second leg left prior to the first leg, which stayed the same (different airline). After many phone calls and lots of patience, new flights were booked on the original dates so that I didn't have to adjust my departing and arriving accommodations in both countries.

So, my tip to you is to book directly with the airline when the budget allows or if the price is only slightly different. But, if there's a significant savings through a third party, pack your patience and allow time for solving these snafus. I certainly stretched my dollar by using Hopper!

The Importance of STEP for U.S. Travelers

The Smart Traveler Enrollment Program (STEP) is a free service that allows U.S. citizens traveling abroad to enroll with the local U.S. Embassy or Consulate. By registering, you provide information about your trips abroad so that the

Department of State can better assist you in an emergency. The program also sends you travel advisories about countries you'll be visiting. For more information, visit travel.state.gov.

I was in Thailand in 2004 when the tsunami killed 230,000 people. Embassies were evacuating their citizens during this natural disaster. Because I hadn't registered with STEP, I wasn't included in the evacuation. Since then, I've made sure to register for all my overseas trips. You never know...

My Travel Currency Cheat Sheet

Whenever I travel to multiple countries, I make a cheat sheet and keep it in my purse. It includes the name of the currency and its equivalent of $10 US. As soon as I land at the destination airport (before I have Wi-Fi and access to Google), I withdraw money from the ATM. Having this prior knowledge helps me know the correct conversion ratio. Only having 100 Rupees instead of 100,000 could be funny, or embarrassing!

My Currency Cheat Sheet for this trip:

Country	Currency	$10 US Equivalent
Mauritius	Mauritian Rupee	441.6 MUR
Réunion	Euro	9.16 Euros
Madagascar	Malagasy Ariary	45,259 MGA
Seychelles	Seychellois Rupee	146.23 SCR
Sri Lanka	Sri Lankan Rupee	3,280 LKR

Maldives	Maldivian Rufiyaa	154.6 MVR
Philippines	Philippine Peso	555.149 PHP
Taiwan	New Taiwan Dollar	317.5 TWD
Papua New Guinea	Papua New Guinean Kina	37.59 PGK
Vanuatu	Vatu	1,200 VUV
New Caledonia	CFP Franc	1,098.68 XPF
Tonga	Tongan Pa'anga	23.808 TOP
Cook Islands	Cook Islands Dollar or New Zealand Dollar	16.69 NZD
Tahiti, Moorea, Huahine, Bora Bora	CFP Franc	1,098.68 XPF

Note: These amounts may change day by day.

The Art of Packing

I vividly remember a college professor telling me, "Less is more." I also clearly remember my dad telling my harried mom as she was packing for a trip, "You know, they have stores where you're going." Both quotes played a role in my packing for this trip.

My goal for this five-month trip was to get all the necessities into a carry-on suitcase plus a daypack as my personal item. With 17 flights, some including multiple connections, there were many opportunities for luggage to get lost. So, by keeping these two containers within my reach as I flew from island to island, I hoped to minimize the possibility of parting with my belongings during my adventure.

So, what got packed and what stayed home? Unfortunately, my fishing gear and pickleball paddle did not make the cut. My compression socks and Trtl Travel Neck Pillow for flying went into the pile. I checked the weather forecast for all 17 islands and considered the cultural dress expectations when choosing my few clothing items to pack. Because I would be on islands the entire trip, I packed shorts, swimwear, flip flops, one dress, and yoga pants. Since the Maldives is mostly Muslim, I included a pair of Capri pants and a wrap for covering my shoulders as needed. It was also the rainy season, so my rain jacket would protect me from getting wet and add a layer of warmth when traveling in mountain regions or cooler islands such as Taiwan.

When choosing which few clothing items to pack, I considered which shorts and tops were interchangeable, which items were favorites that made me happy and were comfortable, and which items could easily be washed in the sink and would hang dry quickly. My footwear choices were important due to plantar fasciitis issues. I packed a black and a blue pair of new Vionic sandals.

I wore my jeans, tennis shoes, and hoodie for the often-cold flights and because those were the bulkiest clothing items that would take up half my suitcase.

I packed all the vitamins and prescriptions needed for the entire trip, plus an extra two weeks just to be on the safe side. This required some pre-planning with my doctor and pharmacy because my insurance company will only fill prescriptions with a 90-day supply. I also researched which countries had a risk of malaria and requested the correct number of anti-malaria pills from my doctor. I asked for the number of days needed, plus enough to start the meds two days before exposure and one week after. I also highly recommend traveling with your prescription to identify what the pills are and why you have a bag full of tablets! I transferred the medications from their large containers to lay-flat sandwich baggies. (Space was everything!) I even fixed the label from my over-the-counter supplements to the baggies containing 161 glucosamine or probiotic pills. (Just in case...) I listed my travel dates on the baggies of meds so if my bag was searched at the airport, it would explain the need for that quantity.

My one frivolous item that I wanted to take along was my small (one and a half foot tall) Christmas tree. That small tree had been on 12 previous overseas Christmas vacations with me. Since my suitcase for this trip had shrunk, I figured my tree needed to shrink too. Off to Joann Fabrics I went to get a tiny Christmas tree. There I found the perfect one. It was tiny and cute as can be! Plus, once Christmas was over, I could leave it behind and make room for a few tiny trinkets to take its place. Win-win.

Preparing My Home for New Tenants

I didn't realize how much I had "spread out" in my home since I moved in six and a half years ago, until I had to start preparing for others to live in it. I began by coming to an agreement with my future renters on what they would like or need for space.

Next came the cleaning and shifting of items to empty dresser drawers and closets. I made many trips to Goodwill when I realized I was storing things that no longer fit or I no longer used. I tucked away computers and locked up files that contained private information. I started concentrating on eating food that I already had in my fridge, freezer, and pantry. I made arrangements with a local food bank to donate any leftover food items the day before my departure.

Then, I printed a list of helpful household instructions about things such as: trash day, the code to the bike lock, important contact phone numbers, and how and when to change the A/C filter. I also included the garage code, the location of spare keys, which recreational items in the garage, such as bikes and beach supplies, were free to use, and anything else of importance.

Mastering Mail Management

Determining what to do with bills, statements, and all of my mail for five months was certainly an issue. I wanted to minimize the amount of bills and statements being mailed to my home, so I set up auto pay with my credit card, mortgage, utility companies, etc. This would hopefully minimize the amount of junk coming into my mailbox weekly. I also kindly asked my renters to open and send me pictures of documents of significance via WhatsApp, so I could take care of them from abroad. Additionally, consider using USPS Informed Delivery, a service where pictures of most mail items are emailed to you daily.

As an extra precaution, I left a few blank checks with a trusted neighbor in case payment to a plumber or A/C specialist becomes necessary. You never know...

Backup Brilliance: Safeguarding Your Travel Plans

What if I lost all the hard work, I did in planning a trip? That's one of my biggest fears. There were dates, confirmation numbers for flights and accommodation, payment information such as how much was paid and how much was due and when, not to mention the names and addresses of those accommodations. There were so many parts to this adventure, I needed some serious organization!

I probably over did it with my backup system, but it works for me, and I sleep well at night with this system in place! Here is my three-tier system:

1. Simplify everything as much as possible and print a copy. For each island I visited, I had one printout of my airfare, one of my accommodations, and a map of the island marking the cool things to do there. I included a copy of the e-visa if one was required. At the end of each leg, I would toss the paperwork and delete the folder.

2. Take a photo of each of these printouts and put them in a folder in your phone's gallery labeled for each island.

3. Email these same photos to yourself or use Cloud Storage just in case something happens to your phone during this trip.

In addition, I made a short version cheat sheet of my entire itinerary as a typed list of confirmation numbers and dates and sent a copy to my mom and sister. In a pinch, they could tell me which airline I was flying or where I was staying. My mom enjoyed following along with my trip via this itinerary.

Travel Tips from My Facebook Crew

I asked my Facebook friends for their best travel tips, and here is the invaluable advice they shared:

- Be kind and engaging. Strike up a conversation with as many different people as you can.
- Learn to say hello, thank you, please, and goodbye in each language.
- Take a few minutes to research local customs before arriving at each location.
- Be safe and enjoy each day and adventure.
- Try one new food or drink in each location.
- Live your dreams because you never know what tomorrow might bring.
- Leave your heart and wisdom wherever your adventurous soul takes you.
- Draw something every day to remind you of your memories.
- Learn one historic reference from each location.
- Immerse yourself in the culture of the communities

you visit and push yourself to experience things unique to the places you visit.

- Talk to the locals about why they love it there; ask them about their history and places to see and what to eat – things that you would not find in guidebooks.
- Do not lose your itinerary!
- Learn something new each day, keep your sense of humor, stay flexible, and always have fun!
- Be spontaneous and soak in every single adventure.
- Be safe and smart.
- Write down every detail each night in a journal.
- Pack light, but with essentials.
- Look ahead to the next stop so you don't miss something you might want to see.
- Make a copy of your passport and leave it with someone in the US.
- Put a copy of your passport and driver's license in your suitcase.
- See all you can, do all you can, and make many friends along the way.
- Live like a local, not a tourist.
- If you get lost and your phone battery is low, change your voicemail to alert others about your location.
- Do not injure yourself overseas. That could ruin the whole trip!
- Enjoy the "now" time at each spot without thinking about the next spot.

Thanks, everybody, for the amazing tips! I told my friends that I would do my best to follow them all. Reflecting on my journey, these tips have been invaluable, enriching my experiences and helping me connect deeply with each new place I have visited.

Follow Me on Instagram

One of my pickleball friends was talking to me about becoming a social media influencer. I explained to her that I'm a retired teacher living on a pension and taking this trip on a tight budget. Once she mentioned that I could someday be paid for my posts, I was interested. When she explained that I might be able to trade social media exposure for free hotel stays or excursions, I was sold! She helped me set up an Instagram account with a goal of 25,000 followers. I immediately started posting travel tips under yvonnes.adventures. Thanks, Loren!

To Book or Not to Book: Navigating Excursions

Deciding whether to pre-book excursions can be tricky. Based on my extensive travel experience, the best advice I can give is, "It depends."

Advantages of Pre-booking:
- Cost and Schedule Certainty: Pre-booking allows you to know the cost upfront and ensures that your daily activities are confirmed.
- Secured Spots: Popular tours and excursions can

become fully booked, so pre-booking guarantees you won't miss out.

Potential Drawbacks:
- Overbooking Risk: Pre-booking everything can lead to a packed schedule, leaving little room for rest or spontaneous discoveries.
- Missed Opportunities: Without pre-booking, you have the flexibility to "wing it" and might find a local guide or driver who can offer a more personalized experience at a cheaper price.

Types of Tours:
- Group Tours: A tour arranged for a group allows you to meet many new and interesting people. These tours often follow a fixed itinerary.
- Private Tours: These tours offer deeper personalization, allowing you to tailor the experience to your interests and pace.

Considerations:
- Preference: Whether you prefer group interactions or personalized experiences can influence your decision.
- Availability: High-demand tours can fill up quickly, so ensuring you have a spot can be a significant advantage.

Information Sources:
- Before the Trip: Research online, consult travel guides, and read reviews to find out what excursions are available.
- During the Trip: Talk to locals, hotel staff, and other

travelers to discover additional options and possibly better deals.

Ultimately, balancing pre-booked excursions with the flexibility to explore spontaneously can provide a fulfilling and enjoyable travel experience.

Travel Insurance for Peace of Mind

I've learned the hard way how important it is to have travel insurance. I'm still paying off an ER visit for a kidney stone while on vacation in California. Now, I maintain an annual travel insurance plan with AIG Travel Guard. For only $259 a year, I have peace of mind any time I travel more than 100 miles from home. It's much cheaper than buying individual policies for each separate trip. You can contact them at 1-800-927-HELP.

Alert Your Credit Card Company Before You Travel!

I once made the mistake of trying to buy an opal necklace, in Australia, by using my credit card. You would think that's not a big deal, but the credit card company did. They put a fraud alert on my card and immediately shut it down! I couldn't even buy a pack of gum, not to mention that necklace I liked.

It's the job of the credit card companies to keep us safe, from unusual purchases, in faraway places, by people unknown. I get that, but it really messed up my trip for two days. So, the lessons learned from that experience were:

1. Always call your credit card companies to let them know where you are traveling and the dates you will be there.
2. Bring a spare credit card.

Because you just never know...

Pack Postcards for a Personal Touch

I know this will sound crazy because you are supposed to buy postcards on vacation, not bring them with you! But let me tell you why...

About 20 years ago, I started writing sincere, heartfelt thank-you notes on postcards from my home state or country. Many times, when I'm traveling and I meet an exceptional guide, the hotel staff goes above and beyond, or I've developed a friendship with the waiters on a cruise, I leave a thank-you note along with the tip. Everyone is touched by such a personalized message from someone they will remember fondly as well.

There's something about postcards that makes them more appealing than notepaper. Perhaps it's the beautiful imagery or the fact that they are a tangible piece of where you come from. This small touch adds a personal connection that a plain note cannot match.

Go ahead, pick up a few of those cute postcards from your area before you head out!

Essential Electronics

I'm no expert, but here's what I've learned by traveling to over 100 countries.

You need to be able to charge your electronics, so research adapters carefully. I found the Hero universal adapter on Amazon for $29. It's supposed to work on all the islands on my upcoming trip, and most importantly, it has two USB ports. I've blown a circuit in a hotel in Amsterdam. I burned up a curling iron in Ireland. I had a dead phone in Uganda. It's important to have the right charging equipment. Sometimes, if I'm unsure, I will grab the correct adapter at the airport of my destination to ensure it is correct.

I must admit that the first time I plug an item into the adapter to charge it, I usually choose the least expensive of my electronics just in case I toast it. When I arrived in Mauritius, I plugged my spare battery pack into the USB port of the adapter, then charged my phone from the spare battery pack. That was just to test the system to make sure it worked properly. Once I trusted it, I charged everything normally. Once burned, twice shy...

Be over-prepared by checking to make sure you have the cables needed for each separate device. For example, my Kindle, phone, and underwater camera each have different charging cables. It's also a good idea to keep a spare charging cable for your phone or tablet to keep it plugged in while on long flights. That way, your devices and spare battery packs are all fully charged when you get to your new destination.

Because I'm an avid reader traveling for five months with only a carry-on, I could not pack paperback books for this trip. Instead, I have a Kindle loaded with over 100 books (thanks, Sue!).

I also chose an underwater camera with rechargeable batteries, so I didn't have to tote a bag full of AA batteries.

I did not pack a laptop or tablet for this trip because I use my phone for basically everything. Personal choice...

Off to Island Hop: The Adventure Begins

Wow, after months of planning, it's finally time to take off. I must admit I'm 95% excited and 5% scared. I've done a teacher exchange to Australia, where I swapped my job, house, car, and cell phone for a year, so I shouldn't be frightened. But this trip is different because there are 17 different islands, flights, and accommodations. There are more moving pieces, so there's more room for error. Hence, the 95/5 split.

Preparations and Goodbyes:
1. Farewell to Friends and Hobbies:
   - I said goodbye to my friends and played some farewell pickleball.
   - I let my bass club know I wouldn't be fishing in any tournaments until the end of May.
2. Family and Itinerary:
   - I sent an updated copy of my itinerary to my mom and sister.
3. Packing Challenges:
   - I packed and repacked my tiny suitcase six times,

trying to decide if I could really live without some of those things.

- I checked in for my flight.

Transition to Renters:

- My lovely renters, Marilyn and Larry, arrived two days before I left so we could hang out together.
- Of course, we were on the pickleball courts 45 minutes after they pulled into my driveway (soon to be their driveway).
- We played cards, answered questions about household things, cooked dinner together, and then they dropped me at the airport with goodbye waves.

Ready or not, the adventure begins!

A Festive Detour Before Island Hopping

On my way to go island hopping, I stopped for a few days to spend Christmas with my family. I arrived in Amarillo, Texas, in the middle of December, where it was cold and dreary. I had only my carry-on suitcase filled with beachwear for the upcoming months. I was wearing my travel clothes: jeans, a T-shirt, tennis shoes, and a hoodie. Luckily, my sister agreed to share her warm clothing with me.

I enjoyed spending time with my brother and his wife one day, then cooking all day with my sister the next. Saturday was the official celebration of our family: eating, joking, and opening crazy Christmas gifts. (My gifts had been delivered on a previous trip to Texas because I knew there would be zero space in my tiny suitcase.) My brother's family drove in from Oklahoma City, and my parents drove in from my hometown of Sunray. After a full day of gorging and visiting, most of us gathered to play cards. I was so happy to get to spend this time with my family.

I said goodbye and I set out for my first island destination. I had a long layover in Denver, where I met up with my good friend Janet for lunch and a walk. Then it was off to Frankfurt, Vienna, and finally Mauritius.

Mauritius

Ok, here's what I learned about Mauritius from Wikipedia, my guides, my driver, and many local people. (Please give me some leeway on exact details).

Mauritius is an island in the Indian Ocean off the coast of Africa and east of Madagascar. It's a very safe (ranked 23rd safest in the world, my mom was happy to learn), friendly, and multicultural place with a population of about 1.3 million people. Most Mauritians live in the five major cities in the center and northwest, while the remaining 220 towns around the island are referred to as villages by many of the locals. Mauritius is smaller than the state of Rhode Island. Mauritians drive on the left side of the road, and horns are used (mostly in a friendly way) more than blinkers. A honk could mean anything from "I want to pass," "You may pass," "You're going too slow," "Watch out, do you see me?", "Do you need a taxi?", or "Hello, my friend." I also noticed that many drivers conserve their A/C and keep the windows rolled down, which also allows for hands out the window motioning for drivers to pass. I saw zero road rage.

24

The island's economy is driven by agriculture, tourism, and textiles (known for their high-end cashmere production). Mauritius produces its own sugar (the United States being one of its top recipients), rum, tea, coffee, bananas, coconuts, pineapples, mangoes, papayas, watermelons, and lychees. I saw giant nets covering entire lychee trees to keep the fruit bats from eating all the profits during the night!

The souvenir shops were filled with cashmere clothing, world-famous Mauritius handmade model ships, and tons of items with the Dodo bird on them. I asked why there were Dodo birds on everything and was surprised to learn the answer. Mauritius was the home of the Dodo bird until it became extinct around 1690, shortly after humans settled on the island. Because the birds previously had no predators, they became lazy and unable to fly. Once people arrived and hunted them for their meat, the Dodos basically couldn't get away and were hunted to extinction. So, when someone gets called a "Dodo Bird" it means they are too dumb to get out of a bad situation. I never knew this...

There is no official language of Mauritius, but I heard English and French being spoken almost everywhere. Mostly, I heard Mauritian Creole, which is a language unique to this island, created by the slaves of the French settlers so they could speak privately among themselves. It was further developed when indentured workers were brought from India to work the sugar cane fields. Indentured workers replaced the freed slaves after abolition in 1835. Kinda sounds like they swapped slavery for slavery to me... just saying.

Locals are proud to announce there is free universal health care, free education up until university level, and free transportation for senior citizens. There are many dogs roaming freely, but they usually belong to people and go home at night. One family I met told me they had 5 dogs, but no fenced yard. The dogs came home when they were hungry.

Mauritius has both a prime minister and a president. The prime minister is the most powerful, while the president is basically a figurehead. Don't shoot the messenger here, just telling you what the locals told me.

Because this island is multicultural, so too is the food. The main local favorites I discovered were dhal puri, chili fritters, curry, and fried noodles with fried egg and chicken. Lots of fish and chicken here! I was certainly missing my beef and pork!

Mauritius was formed about 10 million years ago by volcanic eruptions. I saw black lava cliffs all over the island and took tours to see the most famous volcanoes. The Internet tells me there are four major volcanoes here, but the local guides insist there are 26. You pick...

Some of the most popular activities here include:
- visiting beautiful beaches
- boating on the turquoise ocean
- snorkeling in the crystal-clear water
- fishing in the lagoon or in the deep sea
- booking sightseeing tours
- marveling over the Colored Earth Geoparks

- visiting wildlife parks featuring giant tortoises
- enjoying a local Sega dance performance
- going quad biking or ziplining
- viewing magnificent waterfalls
- receiving a blessing at Hindu temples
- being amazed at the size of the water lilies in the botanical gardens

Yes, I tried to do it all!

Many Mauritians don't travel because it's expensive and "Why leave when paradise is here?"

Lessons Learned by Taking the Bus

The first time I arrive in any location, I watch the locals to see how things are done. Of course, I come prepared with basic knowledge from Internet searches, but the real learning happens on the spot. Here are some things I learned about taking the public bus in Mauritius.

Getting Picked Up

You do NOT have to walk all the way to a posted bus stop sign to be picked up. Just stand anywhere next to the road in a place where the driver can pull to the side to pick you up. You should be standing on the side in the direction he is going. However, if you're on the wrong side and wave him down, he will wait for you to cross the road.

Paying the Fare

Sometimes a helper on the bus will collect the proper bus fare and make change while the driver is driving. No hurries, no worries. Try to keep small bills for this. Other times, there is no helper, and you hand the driver your bus fare as you exit. It is best to give the exact change so as not to hold up progress while the driver makes change. You never know when there will be a helper or not, so stay prepared.

There are no posted route maps or fare charts, so you just have to "know." Ask locals or fellow passengers if you are unsure.

Local Knowledge

As I was leaving my B&B one morning, the owner watched as I got out my 30 rupees for bus fare. She commented, "Aw, you are now a Mauritian!"

Comfort Tips

Learn to sit near an open window in summer! I've had to learn to travel without the comfort of A/C. I have accepted that sweating is part of budget travel.

Getting Off the Bus

Sit near a red button so you can alert the driver when you want to get off the bus. He will stop anywhere when it's safe to pull over.

Patience and Persistence

Pack your patience! Many times, a taxi will pull over when he sees me standing by the side of the road. I tell him I'm waiting for the bus. Of course, he offers to take me instantly to my destination for between five and ten times the bus fare (the price continues to go down each time you say no thank you). It's a personal choice to take the taxi or the bus, but I can stretch my travel money by taking public transportation when it's safe and I have the extra time.

From Strangers to Friends: Bonds Built Through Travel

One of the advantages of solo travel is the invitation it extends to others to chat with you. When you are a couple or with a group of friends, it appears you already have people to converse with, and you become less approachable. There are so many friendly and knowledgeable people in this world of travel! I always pick the brains of my taxi drivers and tour guides, often becoming friends while learning about their country. Often, I will hire the same taxi driver or tour guide at a negotiated price for multiple customized tours.

When I sign up for group tours, there are always people in the group to gravitate toward for chatting. Many times, when I'm hanging out with fellow travelers, I learn from them about new exciting places to add to my bucket list. I also bump into friendly guests if I'm staying at a bed and breakfast because we'll see each other multiple times at breakfast or around the pool.

On this trip, after spending the entire day with my fishing guide (recommended by others), I ended up eating dinner at his home, where his wife prepared the fish we caught. I thoroughly enjoyed the traditional meal and playing with their young child.

When I travel by myself, I always appreciate the opportunity to make new friends and learn from their experiences. It's amazing how much you can discover about a place through the eyes of locals and fellow travelers. Good memories are made this way. Please be safe and cautious when accepting these invitations.

I'm still friends with people I've met on past cruises and day tours! Traveling solo opens up a world of connections and friendships that can last a lifetime. Remember, while making friends along the way is rewarding, always prioritize your safety. This balance ensures your travels are both enjoyable and secure.

Embracing Flexibility: Shifting My Thinking

All I really need to say here is BE FLEXIBLE! I can't tell you how many times I've heard, "If you wanted things to be the same, you should've stayed home." True story.

Okay, a couple of examples for you here. I got off the plane in Mauritius and got some cash from the ATM. I used my currency cheat sheet as a guide to see how many rupees to get since there was no Wi-Fi to Google it on my phone. I bought three bottles of water because I didn't know how long it would be until I made it to a grocery store. Then, I exited the terminal. I had pre-booked an airport pickup through my B&B and even had confirmation. I excitedly looked for my name among the dozens of hand-printed signs held by taxi drivers. I walked the row again, thinking my name was misspelled from Yvonne to Ivan, which often happens. No luck. No worries, I hadn't paid for the pickup yet. So, negotiations began, and I was given a ride via taxi to my B&B.

Now, let's talk about my room. The bedspread was red, the walls were red, the rug was red, and the red hippie beads screamed at me as I entered. Also, the advertised A/C was a ceiling fan. The inside of the fridge was warm and smelly, and I couldn't figure out the TV remote. One good thing: there was a safe so I could secure my passport and important documents for 12 days, except... Ok, deep breaths here... I was told the key to the safe had been lost and it would be perfectly safe to lock my valuables in the wardrobe and nobody would steal them. This was actually true.

It turns out that the ceiling fan was the most powerful ceiling fan in the world, and combined with the open balcony sliders, enhanced the amazing ocean breeze. The warm smelly fridge problem was solved with a quick wipe and flicking the power button on next to the electrical outlet. The TV remote was eventually figured out, but my choices of viewing were limited to Indian and French-speaking shows or the BBC. (I now know all world details because of the BBC). I also shut the TV off and read a lot when I wasn't out gallivanting around. The shower was a different issue: it took one hour to drain yet managed to spill water all over the bathroom floor during my shower. Solution: drop a used towel to soak it up. And that view! All worries about a strangely decorated and somewhat broken room went out the window as I opened my balcony sliders and looked at the beautiful glistening water! Hey, I really shouldn't complain about accommodation at $37 a night with breakfast included!

All things look different when you change the way you think about them.

Discovering Mauritius: Budget-Friendly Excursions

My best and most affordable excursions came from rec-
ommendations by local people for guides and drivers. The
owners of my B&B set me up with Raj, a driver who often works with their guests. Raj and I negotiated a plan for
things I wanted to see and a price that was fair to both of us.
To determine a fair price, I compared what I found on Via-
tor and GetYourGuide. Because he did such a good job on
our first excursion, I ended up having Raj take me on several
more trips around the island.

I wanted to go fishing while in Mauritius but didn't have
the funds for deep-sea fishing. While negotiating with a
local tour guide at Blue Bay, he suggested I try traditional
bamboo fishing, and he knew just the perfect guide to take
me—go figure. So, we negotiated a price, and I headed over
to meet him immediately. What a great experience!

I also found a snorkeling guide and speedboat to Ile aux
Cerfs by meeting Rakesh, a local tour operator who sold
discounted tours from his office under a beach umbrella. I
became a repeat customer of his. Ile aux Cerfs is a small island off the east coast of Mauritius, known for its beautiful
beaches and water sports.

I also passed along the phone numbers of all three of these
tour guides/drivers to people I met during my stay. Win-win
for everyone!

Living Like a Local

Whenever I visit a new country, I want to see everything, do everything, and learn everything. The best experiences happen when you start immersing yourself in the daily routines of a local, rather than just doing touristy things.

For example, by spending 12 nights in the same B&B in Mahebourg, I figured out how to manage many day-to-day tasks. I regularly used the bus to get around and discovered the local custom of "share cabs," where you pay the same amount as bus fare, but multiple people hop in and out of the taxi throughout the drive to your destination. I learned to scoot over in the backseat instead of making new riders enter from the street side. I watched the driver expertly take money and make change without pausing his driving.

I discovered where the two closest grocery stores were, where to buy the best fried noodles, and where to get the freshest fruit. When you get large bills from the ATM, break them into smaller bills when purchasing groceries or meals, so you don't have to pay a bus fare with 1,000 rupees.

When it's raining, there is no need to stay indoors—just grab an umbrella and go anyway. It's too hot for a rain jacket, but an umbrella is perfect. I learned not to freak out when you see a couple of tiny ants in the sugar bowl. Just scoop them out, then put the insect-free sweetener in your tea.

Be kind. Be appreciative. Smile.

Réunion

Réunion is a small island that is 39 miles long and 28 miles wide, lying between Madagascar and Mauritius. It is only a 45-minute flight from Mauritius. Réunion belongs to France. The first thing I noticed upon my arrival in Réunion was that everyone was speaking French. I had a very hard time finding anyone who spoke any English, making it harder for me to navigate the country and its activities, make friends, and even ask basic questions. Here's what I learned about Réunion:

Réunion has no dangerous or poisonous animals on land. However, it is in the "shark highway" between Australia and South Africa, so many sharks hang out here. There hasn't been an attack in three years, but there are many safety rules in place. "Shark Stops," which are buoys with nets, are set up on many beaches to allow swimmers a safe place to play in the ocean. These stops are sometimes removed when the waves are so high that they become ineffective, so people must swim in a different area such as the lagoon.

With a population of just under 900,000, the people of Réunion are known as Réunionese and are proud of it! They are of mixed descent (African, European, and South Asian). Most people here are Catholic.

There are many tourists here, mostly from France, Italy, and Germany. I've met no Americans, and people are surprised when I tell them I'm from the United States.

The currency here is the Euro, and everything is very expensive. I was so spoiled with the cheap prices in Mauritius that I experienced sticker shock when shopping for groceries, looking at menus, and checking taxi prices in Réunion. For example, a taxi from the airport to my Airbnb would have cost over $100! I took the bus instead for only $5.

Réunion is an island of volcanoes and extreme sports. Serious hiking, mountain biking, exploring the lava tubes, horseback riding, river rafting, helicopter rides over the famous Piton de la Fournaise (one of the most active volcanoes in the world), and quad biking are popular activities you can enjoy here. Diving, fishing, and dolphin watching are also offered.

People are kind and often say "Bonjour" and "Merci" when you scoot over to let them pass on the sidewalk. They are also over the top in acknowledging people in crosswalks. Cars will come to a screeching halt if you look like you're thinking about crossing the road. (We could learn some lessons from them!)

My advice if you plan to visit Réunion: pack your patience, learn some basic French, and rent a car. The bus system here is affordable and safe, but it doesn't go into the interior of the country where many of the activities are located. Taking the bus is also very time-consuming with all the necessary transfers.

Let Me Out of Here!

I stayed in an adorable apartment on the beach. My Airbnb host was great about communicating with me via WhatsApp and even met me at the building when I arrived. He showed me the code to the outside gate, gave me the key to the apartment, and asked if I had any questions. All good... UNTIL I decided to go roaming around!

Anyone who knows me knows how geographically challenged I am. Some have joked that I could get lost in a department store or parking lot. (Don't laugh; I've done it!) Anyway, I was diligently making mental notes of my apartment number, floor number, and which way to turn after each landing. Then I came to the tiny, unmanned lobby. I went through a set of glass doors and came face to face with a door with bars. I proceeded to push on those doors. Nothing. Silly me, then I pulled. Nothing. Then I examined my apartment key ring to see if there was anything on it that I needed to scan or insert. Nothing. Then I decided to push and pull harder. Nothing.

Finally, I saw a tiny button with the word "porte" written above it. I don't speak or read French beyond bonjour and merci, but I thought I'd give it a go. Voila! I heard a click and was able to push open the doors of my cage and free myself! In my mind, porte certainly must mean, "Open Sesame!"

Lost in Translation:
My Réunion Island Misadventures

Just when I thought I was breezing through this vacation with absolutely no problems, I hit a brick wall. Between wrong adapters, language barriers, a new tourism staff member, and getting on the wrong bus, I was ready to call a mulligan on the island of Réunion!

When I bought my multipurpose adapter from Amazon several months ago, it appeared to be compatible with the 17 islands I'd be visiting. Well, it worked on the first one and was all wrong for the second one. Oh well, off to the hardware store for a new adapter. Try explaining that to a French-speaking salesman. Good thing I brought an example so he could decipher my needs through hand gestures.

I had a heck of a time getting directions due to my lack of French and their lack of English. I am in their country, after all, so it's on me to figure it out. I started bringing photos on my phone or maps to ask for help. I even started writing down the name of my bus stop or destination in French because my pronunciations butchered their beautiful language. That helped a little.

Next, I visited the tourism office and found a friendly English-speaking associate. Yippee! Well, maybe. Her heart was in the right place, but her skills were basic. After a frustrating hour, I thanked her and then went back to my Airbnb where I had Wi-Fi to finish the bookings and get directions.

The icing on the cake was an unbelievable bus fiasco. I took great pains to print my destination in French on a piece of paper that I showed the driver. He nodded for me to pay and board. Then, as we were approaching my stop, the driver's helper wrote a note which I think said they weren't stopping at my requested destination, but the one before it. No worries, I got off. The next bus came, and I showed the driver my sign with my destination. He nodded yes, and I paid and got on. It was the very next stop, so easy peasy, right? As he was passing my stop, I showed him my sign again and he vigorously shook his head yes. Two stops after my desired stop, he motioned for me to get off. THIS WAS SO NOT MY STOP. Someone explained to me in broken English that I had to walk two blocks to catch the next bus that would take me to where I needed to go. I eventually made it home, but I did a lot of cursing that day! I really wish I spoke French!

Clap Twice to Stop

Learning a new bus system in a foreign country can be quite the adventure. In Mauritius, you could stand just about anywhere and flag down a bus, and it would stop to pick you up. But now, we're not in Mauritius any longer!

Here, there are schedules - tight schedules - posted schedules. There are specified bus stops with no exceptions. If nobody is standing at a specific stop on a route, the bus driver keeps going to stay on schedule. If you want to get off the bus, you must notify the driver by pushing a little red button labeled "stop." These buttons are spread far apart on the bus. What if you're sitting far from a button, someone is blocking your path, the road is too bumpy to reach it, or you're just feeling lazy? You simply clap twice!

I thought my bus driver must have been a mind reader because he knew when to stop without a button being pushed. It also took me a while to figure out why some people were clapping, but others weren't. The next time I wanted to get off the bus, I confirmed with the guy next to me that I should clap twice. And by golly, it worked! I felt a little silly doing it, but hey, when in Rome (or Réunion) …

Crap, I Just Got Hit by a Car!

When asking my friends for advice before this trip, one of my buddies said, "Don't get injured. It could really mess up your trip!" What do you think happened? I got injured.

It happened early one morning as I was walking from the bus stop to the helicopter excursion office. It was quite a walk, and I wasn't sure of the directions, so I flagged down a driver on this sleepy two-lane road. I showed him my flyer with the helicopter picture and the name of the company while pointing straight ahead to ask if I was going in the right direction. (The driver only spoke French and didn't understand English, so a lot of pointing was going on.) After he vigorously nodded that I was walking in the correct direction, I said a quick "merci," then turned around to cross back to the other side of the road. I hadn't even moved away from the side of his car yet when a driver came zipping around from behind him to pass. Because it was a narrow road, there was not enough space for two cars and one person, so his car hit me!

He slammed on his brakes and got out quickly to check on me. There was a lot of panicked shouting in French as the driver began touching my foot, my knee, and my hand to check for injuries. The other driver told him where I was going, so he made me get in, and he drove me the rest of the way. He handed me tissues to stop the bleeding and walked me to the counter of the helicopter place to ask for a first aid kit.

I told him I was okay, and he should go ahead and continue on his way. Other than a few scrapes and a bruised ego, I had no lasting effects from being sandwiched between two cars. I used their restroom to wash my wounds with soap and water. The receptionist offered me some alcohol (not that kind—I don't drink, but I was beginning to think this might be a good time to start) and a couple of Band-Aids. She then proceeded to tell me... (are you ready for this?)...the helicopter flight was canceled. Great, just great.

Persistence Pays:
From Cancellations to Celebrations

I've had two excursions that have given me grief. I really wanted to take a helicopter ride over the famous volcano, and I wanted to crawl through the lava tunnels. I only had one week on this island, so the timing was tight. The tourism office had booked my helicopter ride toward the end of my stay. I made a great effort to learn how to get to the heli-copter base by bus. The night before the flight, I received an email announcing there were not enough people (six need-ed), so the flight was canceled and rescheduled for the next day. Darn.

I had been told earlier in the week that all the lava tunnel tours were sold out. However, I now had a free day, so I took a chance and started calling lava tunnel companies directly to see if there was a single opening anywhere. Bingo! As I was making arrangements, the helicopter company urgently called to tell me that we could go ahead and fly. Great, I knew that was going to be tight and I couldn't make both choices. I chose the flight.

After an hour-long bus ride, I arrived for my briefing for the helicopter flight. Guess what? They canceled it due to bad weather at the last minute. They rescheduled me for the same time the following day. Great.

I immediately contacted the lava tube guide to see if there was still space for me, then hopped on a two-hour bus ride to get there. Wow, what an experience that was, too! I can't believe the horrible luck of a missed helicopter ride turning into enough extra time to make it to the lava tube tour in time! Lemons into lemonade!

I was super excited for my helicopter ride the next day. Then, I got a call saying my 9:45 flight was canceled. How-ever, they would give me an upgraded flight at no extra charge if I could be there by **SIX AM**! Are you kidding me? I checked, and there was a bus leaving my area at 4:40 am, and

I could make it, so I said yes. I think you already know how this next part will go, but I'll go ahead and tell you anyway. As I arrived for check-in at 5:45, they told me the pilot just canceled the flight because of bad weather. Oh my, this was getting ridiculous.

Alright, hang my head and go home, or call another helicopter company to see if they have any spots available. I even guilted the receptionist into translating for me. Voila! One opening at 8:00…so I headed that way. And, wow, was it worth all the trouble it took to go up and see the famous Piton de la Fournaise, one of the most active volcanoes in the world! AND, as a bonus, (yes, I paid a little extra), I got to see the coastline and so many waterfalls! Amazing!!!

The lesson I learned here was:

- Don't always take the word of a tourism office that everything's fully booked.
- Get creative.
- Be proactive.
- Never give up if you really want to do something.

Where there's a will, there's a way!

Madagascar

Wow, after years of trying to visit Madagascar, it's hard to believe I finally made it! I had a ticket purchased pre-COVID, and, well, we all know how that went. Here, in a nutshell, is what I learned about Madagascar.

Madagascar is an island off the east coast of Africa, approximately 1,000 miles long and 350 miles wide. It belongs to the continent of Africa but is its own country, and local people will tell you they ARE NOT African. There is a melting pot of many cultures here. The people of Madagascar are referred to as Malagasy, and there are about 20 ethnic groups across the island.

The capital city is Antananarivo (the locals call it Tana). There are about 20 million people in Madagascar and between one and a half and three million people in Tana, depending on where you stop counting the suburbs. It's crazy crowded, is all I have to say!

Madagascar is one of the least developed African countries. (That explains the intermittent electricity, spotty Wi-

Fi, and hotel amenities that are often broken.) Ninety-one percent of the population lives on less than two dollars a day. My apologies for complaining about electricity and Wi-Fi.

The currency here is the Malagasy Ariary. 4,594 MGA equals one dollar US. The max you can take out of an ATM here at one time is 800,000 MGA (about 175 dollars US). My eyes just about popped out of my head when I plucked that huge stack of bills from the machine. It looked like I robbed a bank!

The two main languages here are French and Malagasy. I have found more English speakers here than in Réunion, but of course, there are millions more people to choose from, so there is that. My driver, Zakaria, told me he enjoys getting to practice his English because he rarely speaks it. Glad I could help!

Madagascar is known for its lemurs (112 different species) and the giant baobab trees. Both lemurs and baobabs are endangered and protected. I was thrilled to see both incredible things.

Here, you drive on the right side of the road, same as in Réunion.

The national dish of Madagascar is Romazava. It's like a hearty stew made with zebu meat and greens. It is served with red rice and a garnish of a tomato and onion salsa-like mixture.

I decided to alter my plans and leave the noise, crowds, and pollution of Tana to experience a different side of this country. I flew to Tulear (aka Toliara) on the southwest coast and headed for Ifaty. I was so happy for the quiet seaside lifestyle here. Everyone greeted each other with "Salama" (meaning peace or all is well) and was super friendly. I was never afraid here.

People get around by Malagasy canoe, pousse-pousse (rickshaw), Zebu cart, or a share van.

I'm so glad my only impression of Madagascar was not just of Antananarivo!

The Food Poisoning Misadventure

One of the last things you want when you're far from home is food poisoning! Well, since I'm basically trying out everything on this vacation, I decided to give that a go too! I thought I was being super careful by only drinking and brushing my teeth with bottled water, ordering drinks with no ice cubes, personally cleaning my own fruit, eating no lettuce or tomatoes on my burgers, and passing on all salads or iffy street food.

Despite my precautions, it happened when I let my guard down.

In an upscale restaurant in Tana, I ordered a local dish made of a hearty stew, red rice, and a topping of chopped tomatoes and onions. Yep, you know what happened next. It started with a rumble, then the knife pains, then the explosion from multiple outlets! This carried on for 28 hours. I remember using the words, "I want my mommy," "I want my own bathroom," and "I want my own bed."

Imodium wouldn't come close to stopping the carnage, so I cracked out the prescription Cipro, a broad-spectrum antibiotic prescribed by my doctor! Don't leave home without it.

Guess who's going to be even more diligent for the rest of this trip?

Change of Plans – From Tana's Turmoil to Tulear's Tranquility

Antananarivo (Tana), the bustling capital of Madagascar, was overwhelming in every sense. It was huge, crowded, polluted, and noisy. Did I already mention crowded? Well, it is the capital city, with somewhere between two to three million people packed closely together. Not my cup of tea. I felt like I had to get out of here! I quickly learned how long it takes to get anywhere inside or outside of the city. I even got estimates from drivers to take me over to the west coast. I was afraid to wander about by myself. I was told to wear my backpack in the front and keep a death grip on my purse and phone. Even when riding as a passenger in a vehicle, I was advised to keep the windows up so thieves couldn't snatch my belongings.

I checked with hotel management, and they only charged me for the five nights I stayed, rather than holding me to my 14-day commitment. Yippee! I booked a flight to Tulear on the west coast and found an adorable bungalow on the water. Ah, peace, quiet, and safety!

Booking the flight and bungalow was surprisingly easy. I used an online travel agency to find and book a quick domestic flight, and for the bungalow, I checked various accommodation websites and read reviews to ensure it was safe and well-rated. Good call on my part. I am especially grateful for the hotel's kindness.

We Lost Power Again?

I've traveled a lot and I know electricity can be sketchy in some countries. But seriously? It's been consistently inconsistent in Madagascar, both in the big city and in my secluded bungalow on the west coast. Even the locals will tell you it comes and goes daily! It happens at the worst times too:

- When I'm sitting in a dark corner of a restaurant and the lights go off. I had to use the flashlight on my phone to see my food!

- Right in the middle of a news story on BBC.

- When I'm trying to charge my electronics.

- When I'm taking a late-night or early-morning shower and the lights go off. Honestly, have you ever tried to shower in the dark?

- When it's stifling hot, and the fan or A/C shuts off.

- Or my favorite, when I've just tucked the mosquito netting (a fine mesh hung over my bed to protect against mosquitoes) all under my mattress and settled in to read my Kindle for the evening, and the lights go out, leaving me in total darkness. That was fun untucking and walking around a dark room trying to remember where I put my reading light. (I really should get an updated Kindle with a built-in light.)

I guess you just get used to it! We certainly are spoiled with exceptionally reliable power back home.

Staying Connected: The Wi-Fi Challenge

One of the hardest things about being away from home is communication. I try to call my mom daily and post my adventures and travel tips on Facebook and Instagram. I also try not to run up a huge phone bill in the process!

Hooray for Wi-Fi, WhatsApp, and Facebook Messenger... when they work!

I chose accommodation with free Wi-Fi to help manage costs. I have an international calling plan with my provider that charges $10 per day to use my phone off airplane mode. But $10 per day adds up quickly! So, I've been trying hard to keep my phone on airplane mode and just use Wi-Fi.

This becomes a problem when the only Wi-Fi signal is in the common areas of my Airbnb, or when it keeps cutting in and out, or when it's too weak to upload my photos. I think I've said, "What's up with the Wi-Fi?" 100 times so far!

I can also be seen in my PJs late at night or early in the morning, waving my phone around on the balcony, searching for a stronger signal. Oh my.

Sometimes, I get tired of being frugal and just take my phone off airplane mode, pay the $10, and get on with my day!

A Heartfelt Fan Find

My friend Deb from Florida messaged me just as I was leaving Mauritius and heading for Réunion. She collects little handheld fans that open and close accordion-style. She asked if I could pick one up in each country when it was convenient. I told her I would be happy to, but she would need to pay postage for me to mail them to her, as there was zero extra space in my suitcase.

The first two fans were mailed. Then, in Madagascar, I was visiting a Baobab Forest, and there were several tables filled with souvenirs. The women were serious about advertising their items. I asked if there was a fan. One woman creatively grabbed a potholder and started fanning her face. I giggled. I showed with my hands the type I wanted. They all shook their heads no.

I went on my one-hour tour of the baobabs. Upon my return, one woman rushed up to me, totally out of breath and grinning from ear to ear. "Madame, Madame, I found a fan for your friend!" She had gone all the way home to get a fan from her house to sell me. She proudly opened it.

I was excited to see the beautiful designs of a fabric Malagasy fan! She proudly twisted it open for me. Rather than a tribal print of vibrant colors as I expected, there was Jesus with the Ten Commandments! Oh my. After she had walked all the way home to get her own personal fan for me, I didn't have the heart not to buy it. So, Deb is getting a fan with a "cool" story!

Exploring Tulear by Pousse Pousse

As I was being driven through the city of Tulear, also known as Toliara, on my way to my new accommodation in Ifaty, I noticed that the streets were filled with tuk tuks/rickshaws. These two-wheeled carts are pulled by a bicycle and a driver with very strong legs! I asked my driver about them. They are called pousse pousse and are the main form of transportation in Tulear. I immediately decided to add it to my bucket list.

Four days later, I set out on my customized tour of Tulear by pousse pousse. My guide negotiated a price for the driver to cart us around for three hours for 10,000 MGA. That's only about $2. A good day for a driver with many customers only brings in $4, so even though I felt a little guilty for the ridiculously low price, he was happy with it.

The ride was very bumpy, and a few times I feared our cart would tumble over when we hit a big pothole. But it wasn't his first rodeo. The driver negotiated all obstacles masterfully. When we came to deep sand, my guide and I would hop out and walk beside the cart and driver until we found firm ground.

We were in sight of Andaboy Beach, referred to by the locals as the "Malagasy Dubai," with one mile of giant dunes not suitable for pousse pousse between us and the beach. Have you ever hiked one mile in deep sand? Our pousse pousse driver took advantage of his free time, removed the seat cushion, placed it on the sand in the shade, then promptly fell asleep. One hour later, as we were returning, my guide started yelling to the driver to wake up so he could brush off the cushion and put the seat back together for us.

I tried not to giggle every time he called, "Poos", "Poos poos", "Hey", "Hey poos", "poosy", "poosy poosy". I thought I was going to die laughing, but I wasn't allowed that outlet! My guide wouldn't see the humor in it, and I had no fellow traveler with me to snicker at his yelling "poosy poosy" at the top of his lungs. It was like when you were a kid in church or school and got the giggles with a friend over something so silly. These are the times I wish I had a travel companion.

The Soft Tinkling Bell: Dinner's Ready

While in Ifaty, I stayed at the Bamboo Club. There were about 20 bungalows with an infinity pool and an open-air bar/restaurant on the beach. The menu was written on a chalkboard and nailed to a tree. If they ran out of something (it is finished), they simply erased it.

I had been eating 90% of my meals here. It was off-season and very slow. Most days I ate alone. To place an order, you simply told the bartender what you wanted and then chilled out by the pool or in a comfy seating area. About thirty minutes later, I would hear a faint tinkling sound from afar. Immediately following the sound, the bartender would call my name and ask me to move to a table in the dining room because my food was ready. He would walk to a nearby bungalow to fetch my hot meal. I never met the person cooking my meals or saw where the kitchen was located. But I was super happy that my bartender had exceptional hearing!

World Cola: A Seaside Offering

While at Andaboy Beach, my guide casually walked away from me. He reached into his backpack and pulled out an unopened bottle of World Cola (the equivalent of our Coca-Cola). He twisted off the cap and stood still for a moment, as if in prayer. Then, he poured a small amount of cola into the sea.

Okay, what the heck was that all about? I had to ask.

This beach is considered a holy place for many local people. They travel here to make offerings to the spirits, hoping to receive blessings in their lives. Why World Cola? Because it is a luxury for them, and it doesn't pollute the water.

Now, I need all the luck, blessings, and good karma I can get. I asked if it could work for me too. The answer was, "Of course, madame." So, I added more cola to the sea. Fingers crossed that it works for me, too.

I Am a Vazaha: Embracing My Wanderer Spirit

When I was in Uganda for a gorilla safari, the local people kept yelling out "Mzungu" while smiling and waving at me. I wondered what they were saying. My driver explained that it is a friendly term used for foreigners or "wanderers." I loved that I was referred to as a wanderer!

Fast forward to my trip to Madagascar. When I heard the word "Vazaha" shouted by many children in the little fishing village just north of Ifaty, once again I was baffled. My guide confirmed that it is a term for strangers or foreigners and almost always means a white person. Nothing mean about it, just stating an obvious fact.

Hi, my name is Yvonne, and I am a Vazaha, a wandering foreigner!

Double the Fare

One of my requests to my tour guide included immersion into non-touristy customs. We visited a local primary school, went to the holy beach for locals, rode in a pousse pousse, and took a shared van.

Now, shared vans are not new to me, but I am always amazed at how many people they can cram into a single vehicle! They also strap charcoal, boards, mattresses, etc., on top of the van. When the person in the front passenger seat was asked to get out so another person could squeeze in to sit on the center console, nobody thought twice about it except for me.

As we were getting out at the bus station to pay, my guide paid the equivalent of $1 for himself and $2 for me. I asked if the price difference was because he's a local and I'm a tourist (locals pay half the price tourists pay for many things here). I probably shouldn't have asked because here's his answer:

"It is because you are bigger. He can squeeze two Malagasy people into the space you took."

Alright, I should have been offended, but Malagasy people are tiny, and it was said so calmly and matter-of-factly that I decided to laugh instead!

An Unexpected Jury Duty Summons

While on my lengthy *Island-Hopping Adventure*, I had a lovely couple renting my home. One of their acts of kindness was to receive my mail and toss 95% of it. If any of the remaining 5% looked interesting, they would snap a photo and WhatsApp it to me so I could deal with it.

I knew something unusual had arrived in the mail when I received a message to call them to talk about a specific piece of mail. I was summoned for jury duty in February. The easy route would have been to have them check a box saying I was traveling and to excuse me, then pop it back in the mail. No such box existed.

I located the email and phone numbers, along with my juror reference number, to contact the county clerk. I returned an electronic request for excusal. I also emailed the county clerk and attached my itinerary and multiple flight documents.

Guess what? Yes, I was summoned for jury duty two days after my expected return date to the United States. I hope I'm not jet-lagged while completing my civic duty!

How Dare You: A Day of Trickery

On my final day in the overcrowded, loud, polluted capital city of Antananarivo, I decided to venture out and see three remaining sites of interest to me: the Photography Museum, the Digue Market (Tana's largest handicraft marketplace), and the Gare de Soarano, the old train station, which was now a building for some upscale shops. I contacted the driver

54

I'd been using during my stay here. He already had clients, but he arranged for someone else to drive me to these three locations, stay with me, and return me safely back to my hotel at the end of the "program."

The "program" was very clear. First stop: the Photography Museum. My new driver's English was very limited, but he clearly said he knew the Photography Museum. So, why did he drive me to the Queen's Palace? His friends were hanging out by the car asking if Madame wanted a guide for the Palace. I said, no, I've already seen it.

Then, he took me to a large, old, historic-looking building with the doors closed. I was deflated because it appeared that my photography museum was closed. My driver assured me it was open, just needed to be unlocked. His three friends quickly ushered me through the front doors. There were no signs proclaiming this building to be the Photography Museum. The three guys stood behind a counter and asked for the admission fee of 30,000 MGA ($6.50) to see the display. I asked where the photos were. They insisted on me paying first. I moved toward the large wooden doors to push them open to see if it was actually a museum. Far in a back corner room, I could see some storage items like the leftovers of an Art Museum that didn't quite make the cut. I immediately turned around and stormed off, telling my driver that this was NOT the Photography Museum I saw pictures of on the Internet!

His response after a failed attempt to squeeze 30,000 MGA out of me for his friends was, "Okay, now madame, we go to the Photography Museum." I was so angry! This guy was supposed to have my back when I went out among the crowds. Instead, he was part of the problem. I was never in danger of being hurt or robbed (or I don't think so anyway), but the little prickles on the back of my neck were highly engaged!

Once we were back in the car and pulling up to the real Photography Museum, I looked him in the eye and asked, "Why did you take me to that place when you knew it was the wrong place? I was frightened. That was just wrong!" My assertiveness surprised him, and he did not have an answer for me.

After I returned to my hotel, I called my original driver and let him know how furious I was! He kept apologizing for the bad behavior of the driver. He referred to him as a "bandit" and promised to call the guy's boss and never use him again for his clients.

Trust your gut...

Bonus Safari: A 17-Hour Layover in Nairobi

What happens when the airline changes your flight, and you have a 17-hour layover in Nairobi, Kenya? You go on safari! Special thanks to my Facebook friends Wendy and Stig for letting me know about Nairobi National Park, which is not far from the airport.

I organized a driver to pick me up from the airport after my flight from Madagascar. I secured a visa, booked a hotel room, and got a good night's sleep. The same driver picked me up at 5:30 the next morning, drove me to the park, and handed me off to Simon, a Maasai guide. I booked my entry ticket online. Cash at the ticket booth is not allowed in an effort to eliminate corruption. (There were signs on the highway announcing "Corruption Free Zone.")

I hopped in the Land Cruiser with my guide, and we were off in search of African wildlife at sunrise. We saw fat crocodiles, grunting hippos, and guinea fowl with blue necks. We also saw a male lion that had killed a cub the previous week because he saw it as future competition! Oh my. The safari drivers were good at calling each other when there was a unique sighting so all the clients could enjoy it.

My favorite animals in this park were the giraffes. I had just read the novel "West with Giraffes" by Lynda Rutledge and had a soft spot in my heart for these beautiful creatures. We were close enough to smell and hear about 20 of them in total. I laughed out loud as they jogged down the muddy road in front of us. It was as if they were in slow motion as their spindly legs flew out from underneath them.

That was a fabulous visit to Nairobi National Park! Because my outstanding guide saw my love for the giraffes, he also took me to the nearby giraffe sanctuary. I was the first customer of the day, so the giraffes were curious and hungry. They would stick out their long, sticky tongues, and I would place a pellet on it. Signs warned not to tease the giraffes with food and withhold it, or you might get a "head butt"! Another great visit!

Then it was back to the airport by 10:30 a.m. to catch my 12:30 flight to Seychelles. Visiting these two parks sure beats the heck out of sitting around an airport for 17 hours!

Seychelles

Seychelles is located off the east coast of Africa, covering an area of about 459 square kilometers (177 square miles). There are 115 islands, but most people live on three: Mahe, Praslin, and La Digue. Mahe, the main island (comparable in size to the city of New Orleans), is the main island, and Victoria is the capital.

The climate is warm and humid year-round. Seychelles has diverse ethnic groups mainly from Europe, Africa, India, and China. There are three official languages: English, French, and Creole. Catholicism is the dominant religion.

Seychelles has a president who is elected by popular vote for a five-year term. The first president was Sir James Richard Marie Mancham, who was beloved by the Seychellois people. He served from 1976 to 1977 and died suddenly, possibly from a stroke.

The currency of Seychelles is the Seychelles rupee (SCR), with 13 SCR equaling $1.00 USD.

Fruits grown here include pineapples, star fruit, mangoes, bananas, papayas, passion fruit, and soursop. Other fruits such as apples and tangerines are imported from South Africa.

Animals found here include the Seychelles domed giant tortoises, fruit bats, tok tok fodies, tenrecs (distant cousins of hedgehogs), and the tiny Seychelles frogs. Unique plants include the pitcher plant, orchids, wild vanilla, and the famous coco de mer palm tree, known for its booty-shaped coconuts.

Tourism is the main source of revenue. Canned tuna exports, offshore petrol, and financial services also contribute to the economy. Driving is on the left, and there is a good bus system. Taxis are available, and there is an unofficial "pirate taxi" system similar to Uber. Ferries run from Mahe to Praslin and La Digue.

I loved my nine days in Seychelles and will definitely return!

Embracing Crunchy Clothes: The Art of Travel Laundry

As part of traveling light and on a budget, I haven't afforded myself the luxury of a laundry service on this journey for two reasons: price and the number of days without my clothes.

I have been washing each day's clothing at night in the sink or shower. Then, I hang them to dry either around the room or, if provided, on a hanging rack outside on the patio. Quick-dry clothes and swimwear are the best!

Most of my Airbnb apartments came with two bath towels, which also need to be hand-washed and line-dried. I've even started investing in a small bag of washing powder in each country so I can get a nice sudsing of my dirty clothes.

I've learned to accept that my towels and clothes will be wrinkled and crunchy! Hey, they're clean!

Renewed Faith in Humanity

I was sunbathing on a lounge chair at a local beach on Mahe Island, surrounded by people who were swimming, snorkeling, reading, and relaxing. Suddenly, the quiet was broken by screams of "HELP, HELP!" At first, I wasn't sure if someone was playing around or truly in distress. Then, I saw a woman far out in the water screaming and knew it was serious. Immediately, we all stood to assess the situation. Three men from the beach ran to the water's edge, dove in, and swam like crazy to get to her. A nearby Stand-Up Paddleboarder grabbed a board and started paddling out to her. An ER nurse on the shore yelled for people to call for an ambulance.

The men pulled an unconscious 82-year-old woman from the water. Her face was blue. The nurse instantly began performing CPR on her. She monitored the patient and reassured the panicked friend that all would be well.

As I watched all the strangers on the beach come together to save a drowning woman, I felt overwhelmed with emotion and started crying. Even though I know CPR, I wasn't needed. Every person who jumped in to help did so from a place of love. Nobody thought about lawsuits if something was done incorrectly, and nobody thought about not getting involved; they just did the right thing!

I later went up to both the first man who jumped in the water and the ER nurse to thank them and tell them I thought they were heroes. They were both so humble about it.

I have renewed faith in the goodness of people!

Navigating Seychelles with Pirate Taxis

Prior to my arrival in Seychelles, I arranged through my Airbnb to have a driver pick me up at the airport and deliver me to my new home for the next nine days. This service was fabulous, and I felt like a queen when I saw my name on a sign being held by a private driver! However much I loved this convenience, I couldn't justify the excessive cost on a regular basis. The airport pickup was 500 rupees, about $34 US, which was quite expensive compared to other options. The bus is only 10 rupees, less than $1.00, but it's time-consuming. You must walk to the correct bus stop, wait, wait, and wait, then, of course, allow extra travel time for all the multiple stops along the way. But, hey, it's only a buck.

On my first day here, I walked into town and got turned around. I was scared, lost, and didn't have a bus pass. In desperation, I decided to hitchhike. A man gave me a ride and introduced me to underground taxis, also known as "Pirate Taxis." He showed me where the pirate taxi drivers hang out while waiting for work.

The next day, I went in search of a pirate taxi. Once I found my guy, we negotiated a price to get me to the ferry dock the next morning for my trip to La Digue. It was about half the price of a regular taxi. I also had him save the date for when I needed a ride back to the airport. All set!

That's how you get around Mahé, Seychelles on a budget!

Andre Knows Everybody!

I was super excited to take the fast ferry from the main Seychelles island of Mahe to the popular island of La Digue. This island is home to some of the most photographed beaches in the world and is easily navigated by bicycle. My Airbnb host had helped me pre-purchase my round-trip, same-day ferry tickets a couple of days earlier. After further research and talking to many people, I decided that I might want to spend more than one day on the island. I threw a change of clothes and my toothbrush into my backpack, just in case. I also checked prices and availability for modest accommodations on La Digue, just in case.

When I arrived at the departure ferry dock (by pirate taxi), I was first in line to see if it was possible to change my return ticket to the following day. Not a problem, less than $2 for the switch! Done.

Upon arrival on La Digue, a very friendly local man rushed up to me and asked, "Madame, do you want to rent a bike?" My response was, "Yes, I need a bike, a place to stay, and someone to take me fishing, please." "Follow me." OK.

He told me his name was Andre and that EVERYBODY knows him! First, we biked to three different accommodations, but all were full. Then, I pulled out my Internet research and showed him two places that were available. He knew exactly where they were! So, I followed him on my bike. Within ten minutes, I was settled into my accommodations for the night, or at least the next five minutes to drop off my things and go exploring.

Andre does know everybody! I later learned, when I was trying to return Andre's rental bike the next day, that wasn't his real name. I kept asking for Andre, and another bike rental guy looked at me strangely, then looked at the label on my rental bike, and said, "You mean James?"

I liked it much better when I thought my hero was named Andre!

A Simple Fix: The Red Plastic Bag

When Andre bid me farewell with my rental bike (he gave me a special rate for two days), I asked about a bike lock. He laughed and said, "No need to lock bikes on La Digue!" Because most people get around by bike here, I figured I'd have a problem picking my bike out of rows of similar-looking bikes. Hmmm.

Flashbacks to when I walked the Camino de Santiago nine years ago (a seven-week trek which started in France and went across the top of Spain). We all put our similar hiking poles in an umbrella stand and our nearly identical dusty hiking boots on a shoe rack outside the albergues each night.

I was a little nervous about someone accidentally grabbing the wrong shoes or hiking poles, so I tied a hot pink shoelace through the handles of my poles and through the loops on the back of my boots. Easy to spot for me, and easily not mistaken by someone else.

I did not have a hot pink shoelace with me on this trip, but I did have a bright red plastic bag holding my snorkel mask. Voila! I tore off a small strip of red plastic and tied it around the handlebars of my bike. Perfect. (This also reminded me of when people tie colorful yarn on the handles of their luggage.)

Hey, use what you've got. I never lost my bike!

The Rooster with a Broken Clock

One day, I needed to get up at 4:30 am to go fishing. I'd been told on several islands that roosters generally start crowing around 5:00 am. So far, mostly true. Imagine my horror when the crowing rooster woke me, and not my alarm. I jumped out of bed, turned on the lights, and said a few bad words. I checked my phone to see how much I had overslept. It read: 3:00 a.m. Seriously? Now, you try going back to sleep after that kind of awakening. Stupid rooster.

Impromptu Michael Jackson Jam

I was waiting at a strange bus stop because I got on the wrong bus. Go figure. I had about an hour to kill before the correct bus would get me home, so I was peacefully reading on my Kindle.

There were about a dozen people quietly waiting at the bus stop when along came a shirtless, very happy, inebriated local. He scanned the crowd, then picked me out personally and started talking to me. Between the accent and the slurring, I wasn't sure what he was saying. Then, he asked where I was from. I said, "USA."

His face lit up, and I clearly understood his next question, "USA, you know Michael Jackson?" He began singing a few unrecognizable lines from a song I assumed was a Michael Jackson song. Then, the funniest thing happened. A very sober 30-year-old guy, also killing time waiting for a bus, started singing along with the drunk guy. This, I understood, and even joined in for a few lines. The young guy told me he was a huge Michael Jackson fan and sang a few lines from some of his other songs.

Next, because the whole scene was kinda funny, I asked the young man if he could dance like Michael Jackson. So, the sober guy and the drunk guy both showed me their best moonwalk. I was laughing and applauding at the same time.

Halfway through this entire scene, an older, distinguished local man with a cane, a silver ponytail, and big turquoise rings on his fingers joined our motley crew. He didn't say a word, just smiled quietly to himself as he witnessed our interaction with the Michael Jackson fan. The next bus arrived, and the young guy, distinguished gentleman, and I got aboard (drunk guy stayed behind).

I was still smiling about what had just happened when three stops later, the distinguished gentleman got off the bus.

He turned around and looked right at me up in the window. I waved, and his face broke out in a huge smile. We shared a moment over Michael Jackson.

Just think, I would have missed this entire comedy show had I gotten on the correct bus!

Learning How Cinnamon and Nutmeg Are Grown

My Airbnb host and I walked to a local spice garden. She pointed out many plants and their uses. I was impressed with the locals' use of lemongrass in tea to ward off mosquitoes. If I were planning to stay in Seychelles longer, I would need to acquire a taste for fruity teas. I was most impressed with how cinnamon and nutmeg are grown. I had no idea!

Cinnamon trees produce two things we use in cooking. Cinnamon oil can be extracted from the leaves, which are also used in cooking and making tea. The cinnamon I'm most familiar with is ground cinnamon from cinnamon sticks. I've never really thought much about it, but it's quite time-consuming work! First, the branches are cut at an angle to not harm the tree. The outer bark is scraped, and the branch is soaked. This process, known as "peeling cinnamon," involves carefully removing thin layers of the inner bark, which instantly curl. Then, the cinnamon is dried.

Nutmeg is also grown in Seychelles. The nutmeg tree produces a fruit slightly larger than a golf ball. The outermost layer can be used in making jam or candy. The dark hard seed in the center is encased in bright red netting called mace.

Mace can be peeled off the seed, dried, and used in cooking as a more delicate spice. Ground nutmeg, which I put on my holiday eggnog or in my homemade pumpkin pie, comes from grinding the hard inner seed.

I will never complain about the cost of these spices now that I know how much work goes into producing them!

The Coco de Mer - Nature's Naughty Tree

Seychelles is home to a very famous tree. It is so famous that the souvenir shops all sell products in the shape of its very suggestive fruit! It's the Coco de Mer palm tree. This palm tree takes 25 years to even begin producing fruit, then seven more years for that fruit to mature. What's so famous about this fruit? The female tree produces a sort of double coconut that strongly resembles a woman's buttocks. You can buy soap, magnets, keychains, statues, etc. in this shape, "butt" you MUST have a permit to have a Coco de Mer fruit in your possession. These trees are protected.

Want to know what else is unique about Coco de Mer? The male tree produces a fruit resembling a very excited part of the male anatomy. Yes, Mother Nature does have a sense of humor!

Everything Happens for a Reason

As an avid fisherwoman, one of my goals is to try local fishing on different islands. So far, I've tried bamboo fishing in Mauritius, tourist fishing from a fancy boat in Réunion, and hand line fishing from a Malagasy canoe in Madagascar.

I set out to try fishing in Seychelles. I asked many people who referred me to tourist companies offering very expensive half- or full-day experiences. I couldn't afford any of them on my budget. I kept questioning people, asking about the possibilities of finding a local fisherman to take me out for a traditional fishing experience.

Then, I met Dylan. Everybody told me Dylan was a good fisherman. We negotiated a price, and we agreed to meet at the helipad beach at 6:00 a.m. the next morning (me on my bike and Dylan in his boat).

I showed up, but Dylan never did. I texted, but there was no response. I called, no answer. So, I rode my bike to the nearby plantation where Dylan works.

Dear Marie was working at the reception desk at this early hour. I told her my story. She said she'd call Dylan. No answer. So, I left in search of a local fisherman to take me fishing.

Fifteen minutes later, I got a call from Marie. She knew a local fisherman who would take me fishing for half a day. Meet him at "the church" in 20 minutes. I asked her how I would recognize him. Her response was, "You'll know him when you see him."

Sure enough, here comes a man on a bike pulling a small cart with one fishing rod and a gas container. Meet Louis, my new fishing guide! He put gas in the boat, and off we went.

We tried trolling for an hour with no luck. Then, we went "old school." We cracked out the hand lines and fished 30-40 meters deep using cut-up fish for bait. I only caught two fish, but we had a blast!

I asked Louis how he knew Marie at the plantation. They both worked in the same school previously. I told him I was a retired teacher. I later called Marie to thank her for the fishing guide setup, and we chatted for a bit, teacher to teacher. I told her I was glad that Dylan stood me up so that I could meet her and Louis.

Marie told me, "Yvonne, everything happens for a reason." Amen to that!

Tracking Down the Pitcher Plant

Anytime I travel to a country with unique plants or animals, I put it on my list to see them. In this case, it was the pitcher plant that I just had to see! After several attempts at botanical gardens or on local hikes, I found an advertised area known for having pitcher plants.

I set out on this small hike with only a picture from the Internet in my mind of what I was looking for. Nothing. Then more nothing. Luckily, I stumbled upon a sign with a map directing me to their exact location. I dodged some low-hanging branches on an overgrown trail, and then, BAM, there they were!

Wow, they were bigger than I thought and a beautiful yellow. After reading the sign about them, I discovered a little flap on top of the plant, which acted like an umbrella. The sign also said that this flap contained a scent that attracted insects. There was a liquid deep at the bottom of the plant that served two purposes: first, to drown the bugs, and second, to digest them! What an amazing plant! I'm so happy to have seen them in the wild.

The Snorkel Mask Reunion

Earlier in my trip to Seychelles, I witnessed a near-drowning. That same day, as I was going to purchase a snorkel, a friendly German lady loaned me her full-faced snorkel mask. While I was snorkeling with the borrowed mask, I found another snorkel mask on the ocean floor. Since I knew there was a possibility it belonged to the people rushing off to save their friend or one of the hotel guests, I gave my WhatsApp number to the guy renting out the beach equipment. He contacted me five days later and said the woman was released from the hospital and was checking to see if anyone had found her mask.

We all began communicating with each other. The friend of the lady who nearly drowned met me at the church. I gave her the snorkel mask. She said her friend had a mild heart attack, but everyone acted so quickly that they saved her life! She was in the hospital for four days, then released and back to swimming again. She wished she knew who the ER nurse was. Well, she was in luck because I had taken a picture of this hero! I texted it to my new friend, and she was going to show it around so they could locate her and thank her.

We hugged each other, and she invited me to visit her home in France. You never know, I might just take her up on it someday!

Reluctant Farewell to Seychelles

I loved, loved, loved my time in Seychelles. I wish I had spent less time in Madagascar and more time in Seychelles, especially La Digue! Seychelles even passed Mauritius to take the #1 spot of my trip so far. I can't put my finger on just one thing that made it amazing, but here are a handful of reasons I loved Seychelles so much:

- Crystal clear turquoise water
- Perfectly warm water for swimming
- Gigantic boulders on the beach
- Soft white sand
- Friendly people
- Most people speak English
- Everyone was helpful
- I felt totally safe here
- Groceries, accommodations, and transportation were affordable
- Gorgeous views from so many places

Seychelles, I'll be back! And did I mention the beautiful turquoise water?

Sri Lanka

Sri Lanka is a mango-shaped island in South Asia in the Indian Ocean. It is about the size of West Virginia. Colombo is the capital and largest city. Sri Lanka was known as Ceylon until 1972. The name Ceylon is kept on famous items such as their tea. Sri Lanka means "Resplendent Island." There are about 22 million people here.

Sinhala and Tamil are the official languages, but English is spoken everywhere. This is a very affordable destination with budget accommodations, food, and transportation. The currency here is the Sri Lankan Rupee. $1.00 = 313 Rs or LKR. Sri Lanka is famous for Ceylon tea, gemstones, rubber, coconut, and exotic spices.

The religions here are Buddhism, Hinduism, Islam, and Christianity (in that order). There is a president and a prime minister. Driving is on the left. You can travel by car, train, bus, taxi, tuk-tuk, or motorcycle (helmets required).

Portuguese, Dutch, and British influences are seen throughout the island. Foods to try here are egg hoppers, rice and curry, milk rice, buffalo curd, dhal curry, crab, prawns, and pani pol. Be aware that Sinhalese people like their curries very hot!

Animals on this island include elephants, leopards, many species of birds, and 3 million "street dogs."

Sri Lanka is one of the happiest places I've EVER visited! Smiles and hospitality are world-famous. The guides and drivers were always asking, "Are you happy, Madame? If you're happy, I'm happy." So eager to please. There are many cultures living together in peace. Don't be surprised if you get invited into someone's home for tea!

Navigating Sri Lanka with Uber Tuk Tuk

Prior to my arrival in Sri Lanka, I had been advised to take a taxi to get to my hotel and was even told the maximum price to pay. I went straight to the taxi counter and was quoted double the price! I told them what I was willing to pay, and they said I needed to go outside the airport onto the sidewalk and catch an Uber Tuk Tuk for that price.

I did! Over an hour in a bumpy tuk tuk with my suitcase and backpack made a comical sight, I'm sure. But what a way to see this new country! Fresh air, wind in my hair, honking, jostling, side by side with other tuk tuks—it was just right for me! And the price was right, too.

Once at my hotel, the staff advised me to put the Uber app on my phone. That way, I would always know the correct cash price to pay without having to haggle (even though I love haggling). I could choose a motorcycle, tuk tuk, or car for transportation at the different listed prices.

I used this method for my entire stay in Sri Lanka! I never had to wait more than two minutes for a tuk tuk to show up at the curb. Great system! I was grateful the taxi counter pointed me to this option.

Mangosteen: The Queen of Fruits

When I'm in a new area, I always try the local foods. I saw these dark red, purplish round balls at a fruit stand and asked my guide about them. He seemed surprised that I didn't know about mangosteen. So, I bought three of them (expensive compared to other fruits) and decided to give them a go. To get to the fruit inside, you squeeze the outer shell until a split forms, then pull apart the outer covering. (Fancy hotels will use a knife to cut the outer shell for a classier presentation.) Inside, there are small, white, fleshy segments, like little tangerines. Pop the little segments into your mouth, and wow! They are incredibly sweet and juicy. I've never tasted anything quite like it!

Mangosteens are known as the "Queen of Fruit" or a "Super Fruit," and I know why! Now, they are one of my all-time favorite fruits! I discovered that there are different levels of sweetness and firmness based on the exterior color: red means firmer and not as sweet, whereas dark purple means less firm and sweeter. You must try them! I hope I can find them in the United States. I was told to look for them in the Asian markets when I return to the States.

Fishing on Stilts - A Unique Sri Lankan Tradition

As I was researching things to see and do in Sri Lanka, I saw incredible photos of Sri Lankan men sitting on stick chairs in the ocean, fishing from these perches. I learned that these are the famous stilt fishermen of the southern part of the country. How unique! I asked my driver if we could include that stop in my program. "But of course, madame."

We arrived in the late afternoon, which is not prime fishing time, but it was prime time for tourists to give it a try. Of course, there is a small fee for this. First, you leave your shoes on the beach. Next, try not to get your shorts wet as you walk out into the water to the designated perch. The water is not very deep, and there are no big waves, making it easy to wade out. Then, climb up the homemade rungs (be careful because the bottom rung is slippery with moss). Once you are balanced, you will be handed your stick fishing pole, complete with line, sinker, and a tiny hook baited with a smidgen of shrimp. Dangle the line in the water until you feel a tug. Then, lift quickly to set the hook!

I caught a tiny sardine while I was testing this out. Everyone was surprised and declared, "You are very lucky, madame!" That, I am!

Getting down from the perch was less graceful.

These stilt fishermen usually fish for one to two hours every morning, then sell the fish they catch at their roadside stand. Because they have become famous here, they supplement their income with tips for posing with tourists who want to give it a try. Very cool.

Speedbumps on the River

I took a 90-minute tour of the Madu River by boat. The Madu River in Sri Lanka is about 150 meters wide in some areas and is home to a diverse array of wildlife. Tourists often spot monkeys, monitor lizards, and a variety of bird species along the lush, green riverbanks. There were probably 50 boats filled with tourists doing the same thing. How do you control the speed on a river with so much traffic? River speed bumps!

Along the route, there were buoys on either side of the river with a thick rope stretched between them. The first time I saw the guide approaching this rope, I cringed. That'll mess up your prop! Nope. The guide slowed down, lifted his motor slightly out of the water, just enough to clear the rope. He dropped the motor back down and continued down the river without a second thought. I saw all the other boats doing the same thing at all these strategically placed "River Speed Bumps." Clever.

Street Dogs of Sri Lanka

One of the first things I noticed in Sri Lanka was the huge number of stray dogs. They are called "Street Dogs," and there are about three million of them. Most are medium-sized, tan, and friendly. People walk among them, and cars drive around them as they cross the street or even sleep in the middle of the road.

I asked several local people about the dogs. The "Street Dogs" are fed daily at designated places that provide dog food and scraps. The dogs are always given any leftovers—no food goes to waste here. There are so many that it would be impossible to get them off the streets into adoption situations, so the street is their home. Government agencies try to vaccinate as many as possible to reduce the risk of diseases and rabies. A dog wearing a red collar has been vaccinated. Neutering is also done to keep the numbers under control. If an animal has a little "v" taken out of the tip of its ear, it has been neutered.

I never felt afraid of any of these dogs as I walked through them. They all seemed friendly. I did not pet them, though, because I was unsure of the level of care they had received and was unwilling to take a chance. I donated a lot of leftover food to these grateful fur babies.

I know a handful of friends who would have a hard time seeing all these street dogs roaming freely. They would want to take them home and pamper them.

What Exactly Is Curry?

I'm going to play my "blonde card" now... During my tour of a spice garden, I asked my guide if curry came from a leaf, nut, or fruit. He was surprised at my question, and I felt a bit embarrassed, not wanting to appear stupid by asking. He didn't give me an answer and just continued with the tour. As with many things on this journey, I decided to "Google" it when I got back to my Airbnb. Here's what I learned about curry:

There is a curry plant, which has silver-grey, needle-shaped leaves and emits a curry scent. It is purely ornamental and has nothing to do with cooking. There is also a curry tree. Its leaves are oval-shaped and can be dried and added to dishes for a subtle aroma and flavor.

Curry powder is made by mixing a variety of spices such as turmeric, cumin, ginger, and black pepper. Other ingredients such as garlic, cinnamon, chili pepper, curry leaves, mustard seeds, fennel seeds, cardamom, nutmeg, cloves, dried basil, poppy seeds, and saffron may be used. It is often a golden color.

I am not a fan of spicy curry, which is a shame, because Sri Lankans like their curries hot!

Thanks to Google, I now know all about curry!

The $50 Fishing Fiasco

I've been looking for opportunities to fish with the locals in each country on my adventure. In Sri Lanka, I was told Negombo was the place to do that. I asked my driver to help me find a fishing guide.

We decided the best place to find a fishing guide was at the fish market where the fishermen were selling the catch of the day. I stated that I'd be willing to spend $50-60 for three hours of fishing.

After my driver spoke to several fishermen in the local language, he told me we had success. We were to meet at the dock at 7:00 am the next day. That sounded cool to me, even though I didn't understand a word of Sinhala.

The next morning, my driver and I met the fisherman at his fishing boat, which turned out to be a six-seat tour boat. No problem, I put my bag in a seat instead of the wet bottom of a working boat.

We set out. The guide asked if I wanted a tour before fishing. I said, "No, three hours of fishing, please." First, we needed to stop for gear and bait. What? This guy was not prepared. During the stop, he handed the collapsed rod and reel to a friend who proceeded to string it incorrectly. I stopped and assisted him. Oh no, this is not looking good.

The guide came back in 10 minutes with a tiny cup of shrimp for bait and a small, wadded receipt with hooks in it. Off we went out into the lagoon where he saw a man throwing a net. We started there. I caught two small fish, and the guide was beyond excited and came to the front of the boat to pose with me and the fish. I had hoped we would catch bigger and more fish than that!

He asked, "Are you happy? We go now?" We drove around for an hour and barely fished for an hour. I asked for one more hour, please. This was a three-hour fishing trip, right?

Next, I broke off a hook on a rock. I handed the line to the guide, and he handed me the paper with four hooks. "You do it, Madame, I don't know how." I couldn't believe it—a fishing guide who didn't know how to tie on a new hook. We were in trouble.

Shortly after that, I broke off a hook and the sinker when I got snagged on another rock. I asked the guide for another sinker. "No, Madame, I only bought one." At that point, it was clear we were finished.

I concluded that our guide was not a fishing guide at all. He just had access to a boat with his job and couldn't pass up $50.

Hey, it made for a funny story anyway. You might as well laugh about it!

The Symphony of Fresh Bread

Across Sri Lanka, in the big city of Colombo and in the smaller cities like Galle, Sigiriya, and Negombo, I kept hearing a familiar tune. I couldn't quite place it and hadn't yet made a connection as to why they were playing it. So, I asked my guide.

He said that when you hear that music, it means the bread truck or bread tuk tuk is driving around selling freshly baked bread and other bakery items. At that moment, I connected the tune with the delivery of fresh bread. So, I flagged one down and bought something. The bread I bought was in a flat, coiled ring with a slight buttery yellow color. It was divine! It tasted a bit like the Hawaiian rolls we can buy in the States.

And the tune they all played? It was Beethoven's Für Elise. Every time I hear that specific piece, I now think of fresh bread! Yum!

A Roller Coaster Train Journey

While visiting the city of Ella, my guide took me to see the Nine Arches Bridge. Beautiful! On top of the bridge runs a railroad track. We walked along the tracks until the local tourism police announced that a train was coming, and we must clear the track. We all stepped back and watched with excitement as the train clicked by us and its passengers waved out the windows. What an event!

Then and there, I decided to ride that train while in Sri Lanka.

Three days later, I was on board the train from Colombo to Kandy! Nobody warned me how rickety, jerky, and bumpy the ride would be. Oh my! Imagine windows open, fans blowing, no A/C, vinyl seats, and a roller coaster ride with no pull-down bars. Now you know...

I did manage to get up and walk around to take some pictures of the beautiful countryside. Many people were standing in the open-air section between the train cars to take photos. A guide showed us how to lean back over the tracks with one leg stretched backward for a daring photo. Thanks, but no.

I'll probably need a chiropractic adjustment, but I'm glad I rode the famous "Train to Kandy"!

Connecting Through Pickleball in Sri Lanka

When I'm at home in Florida, if I'm not fishing, I'm playing pickleball. While on vacation, I Googled pickleball on each island. Bingo!

I communicated through WhatsApp to find the newly opened Pipinya Pickleball facility in Colombo and immediately got a response from the owner. What a nice guy! I explained that I not only needed to borrow or rent a paddle but also needed three people to join me.

He set a time and reserved the court for me for two hours. When I arrived via tuk-tuk, I immediately felt like I was home in Florida. The locals were so happy to have a chance to play with an experienced player.

We played seven or eight games and kept switching it up to keep the play even. So much fun!

I wished them luck and told them I hope pickleball takes off in Sri Lanka the way it has in America. I smiled all the way back to my hotel!

Farewell to the Land of Smiles

During my ten days in Sri Lanka, I noticed that everyone was smiling! If I said hello, their faces would light up as they greeted me in return. If I waved out the window of my tuk-tuk, car, or train, they would smile and happily wave back. Nobody looked at me with suspicion, trying to figure out why a foreigner was waving or saying hello.

I will miss the genuine smiles in Sri Lanka!

Maldives

The Maldives is a country consisting of 1,192 islands in South Asia, located in the Indian Ocean. Of these, 187 islands are inhabited. It is the smallest country in Asia by land area. The name "Maldives" is derived from its capital city, Malé, and translates to "the islands of Malé," with "dives" meaning islands. The island of Malé itself is 8.30 square kilometers (3.20 square miles) in size, while the smallest islands are mere sandbanks spanning a few hundred square meters. The total population is approximately 517,887 people.

The official language is Dhivehi, but English is commonly spoken. The currency is the Maldivian rufiyaa, but US dollars are widely accepted, with an exchange rate of $1.00 USD to 15 MVR or Rf. Driving is on the left. The Maldives has a president and a vice president, with the president elected by the people for a five-year term. The primary sources of income here are fishing and tourism.

All the citizens in the Maldives are Muslim. Women must cover their arms, legs, hair, and neck to enter a mosque. Shoes are removed and left outside. My guides advised me not to walk in front of praying people while taking photographs. Selling alcohol is illegal here, and pork is not available on the island. If you enjoy fish and chicken, you are in luck!

Tea and coffee are popular beverages. I often saw small groups of men drinking coffee together at sidewalk cafes throughout the day. I couldn't get enough of their delicious cardamom and chai teas!

In contrast to Sri Lanka, where there are millions of street dogs, the Maldives has an abundance of street cats that are regularly fed by the people. When I asked about the absence of dogs, I was told that dogs are considered unclean by Muslims and are not allowed in the Maldives. Despite this, I love both dogs and cats!

One of my favorite aspects of the Maldives was the variety of water activities available! They offer scuba diving, snorkeling, kayaking, parasailing, wakeboarding, windsurfing, jet skiing, kitesurfing, flyboarding, fishing, and more. I wanted to try flyboarding but chickened out.

I loved the Maldives and will certainly return!

Morning Fitness in Paradise

The Maldives is home to many islands, and I chose to make my base in Hulhumale for ten days, taking excursions from there. It turned out to be a wise decision.

My hotel was located right on the beach, facing east. Every morning, as part of my daily ritual, I walked along the beach, watched the sunrise, and collected beautiful seashells.

I was not the only person enjoying this start to the day! There were three groups of Muslim women, fully covered, using pool noodles for informal water aerobics classes. Different age groups of children participated in swimming lessons. Many people, both tourists and locals, were out for a morning walk, while several men were regular joggers. My all-time favorite group was the older men, kinda heavy, being led by a buddy instructor in "Biggest Loser" style exercises on the beach. There was a lot of grunting and groaning from this group, but the leader always managed to wish me a good morning.

I loved, loved, loved the morning exercise mentality of the Maldivian people! The sense of community, the diversity of activities, and the dedication to health and well-being were truly inspiring. It was a beautiful way to start each day, surrounded by people from all walks of life, united by the simple joy of being active in such a stunning setting.

Rays of Delight

I love snorkeling, and islands with crystal-clear turquoise water call my name. I signed up for a snorkeling trip through my hotel and got a real treat. We were just paddling around, enjoying the basic zebra-striped fish and unicorn fish, when we looked down and saw stingrays. Lots of stingrays. Suddenly, the stingrays came up to greet us!

I've fed stingrays in the Caribbean, where you stand in knee-deep water and wedge a bait fish between your fingers. The stingrays glide over your hand and gently take the fish.

That was fun, but being fully immersed in the water with stingrays all around you is a whole different ballgame!

They were below us, next to us, touching us, swimming so gracefully it looked like they were flying underwater. And they felt so soft and velvety smooth. These are wild animals, and I could see their barbs. I had to trust the guides when they told us we'd be okay if we didn't do something stupid like trying to ride them or restrain them. They are unafraid of people because they get fed and are used to so many people in the water.

I loved this surprise so much that I booked that snorkel trip three times! Pretty darn cool!

Villingili: A Journey Off the Beaten Path for 20 Cents

After my daily beach walk and breakfast, I caught a 90 MVR ($6 US) taxi to the Malé ferry terminal. I only paid 3.25 MVR for a ferry ride to Villingili—that's 20 cents! This is most likely the cheapest thing I'll do on my entire vacation. The ferry was filled with locals who were trying to figure out why a foreigner was on their ferry.

Once I got to the island and discovered it wasn't a tourist destination, I understood the price and the stares. Most people who live on Villingili take the ten-minute ferry ride to work in the busy city of Malé. Then, they repeat the process to return to their peaceful island at the end of the day.

I made the most of my day trip by popping into the one store that was open, which offered a huge variety of local products. I ate in a local café, chatting with locals at near-by tables. Finally, I spent some time reading my Kindle on the public beach, enjoying a solitary and peaceful experience. Then, I hopped back on the 20-cent ferry back to Malé.

What a peaceful, cheap, and non-touristy kind of day! It was quite the break from my busy days.

Learning to Fish the Local Way

As I mentioned before, my hotel in the Maldives was right on the ocean, so every morning, I took a beach walk. While picking up seashells and watching the beautiful sunrise, I usually ran into my new fishing buddy, Rafiya. Twice, he let me try fishing with his fixed rod rig with a set amount of line. He even showed me how to dig worms for bait out of the sand. I did not have any luck either time but wanted to try on my own without borrowing his gear.

I found a fishing tackle shop near my hotel and showed the guys a picture of the rig Rafiya was using. I walked out of the store with my very own extendable rod, line, five hooks, five sinkers, and a pair of little pliers for $10. What a bargain!

The next morning, I was all set to try fishing on my own. I dug out some worms, waited for the tide to go down, then started tossing the line with a piece of worm on it, and gently jigging it back. I caught two little fish on my own. Then my buddy Rafiya appeared. He had come to give me some beautiful shells he'd found while octopus diving. Although he was dressed for work with no intention of fishing, he stayed for four hours showing me how to dig for sand fleas.

Man, the fish went crazy for them! I caught three more fish on the sand fleas! That was super fun.

I bid Rafiya farewell and took the fish back to my hotel, giving them to a worker at the reception. Later that evening, the manager of my hotel and one of his friends showed me how to go sunset fishing in the ocean from the shore. This was a totally different way of fishing. We each had an empty water bottle with fishing line wrapped around it. A piece of coral was tied near the end to work as a sinker. We put a tiny bit of cut-up squid on the tiny hook.

Watch out, people behind me, because I kept the bottle in my left hand and the line in my right. I wound up and hurled the weighted end as hard as I could and let the fishing line spool off the water bottle. At first, it didn't go very far, but after multiple tries, it was just like casting with a spinning rod.

I got pretty good at it and even caught a small fish! My fishing instructor caught a red snapper, which he kept and later cooked for my dinner at the hotel café.

I truly appreciated the opportunity to learn from these kind and friendly locals. What cheap and fun fishing experiences, old school style!

Enchanted by Maafushi

While in the Maldives for a week, I not only enjoyed the beach in front of my hotel daily but also took some day trips to explore other nearby islands. The island I loved the most was Maafushi! My recommendation to you when you visit the Maldives: skip Malé, skip Himmafushi, skip Villingili, and spend a week on Maafushi. Why?

Maafushi is only a 45-minute ferry ride from Malé Airport. It has many nice resorts and enough water sports and beautiful beaches to keep you busy every day for a week. For those who love shelling, there are plenty of beautiful seashells. The island is dotted with tree swings and has pristine, white sandy beaches.

If you want excitement, go jet-skiing, parasailing, or try your hand at the unique flyboard. If you prefer calmer activities, rent a kayak, bicycle, or paddleboat, or go for a beach walk. If you really want a slow pace, read a book or take a nap in any of the many resting spots on the beach.

You could not possibly get bored on Maafushi!

The Frustrating Fellow Traveler

Have you ever met **that person** who drives you crazy by implementing every single one of your pet peeves? I met her on this excursion. At first, she looked like an average European traveler in her mid-30s. She was friendly and seemed to be having fun. However, she was extremely disorganized. Because I take pride in being punctual and "ready," I sometimes get annoyed when others don't show the same respect when in a group. I know we all get a pass now and then, and none of us is perfect, but this lady hit all the negatives.

We were on a snorkeling excursion booked online. Some of us prepaid by credit card, while others needed to pay in cash upon arrival. It was also noted that if you wanted to purchase the videos of your snorkeling experience, you needed to bring $10 in cash.

The day started with the taxi picking us up at our hotels. I had my breakfast early so I could be in the lobby 15 minutes prior to pick up, as requested by the tour company. My driver finally showed up 15 minutes late and was aggravated because the person to be picked up before me wasn't ready on time. After I got into the taxi, we had to return to the original hotel to see if she was ready yet. This is when I met "Pet Peeve Girl" (PPG). She offered no apologies for her tardiness, and we hurried off, hoping the ferry wouldn't leave without us.

Ready for this? Next, she asked the driver to find an ATM and stop so she could get cash to pay for her snorkeling excursion. Seriously? He's anxious now because he has a schedule to keep as well. He said he would drop her at an ATM, then get me to the ferry, and go back and pick her up and take her to the ferry. I thanked our driver for his consideration. We eventually all made it onto the ferry in time.

But it didn't end there. Our first stop was the sandbar. Each guest (except for one) put their phone into the guide's waterproof bag so they stayed dry on our swim to the sandbar. We were given our phones back when we were on the sandbar. Off we each went to take photos and enjoy our time. I was snapping photos of the crabs, turquoise water, and seashells when PPG asked if I'd take some photos of her. No problem, and I stuck my hand out for her phone. Her response, "Oh, I didn't feel like bringing it to the sandbar. Can you use your phone and send them to me?" Normally, I'd be the first to volunteer to do this for someone, but I was not feeling like a nice person at that moment. I suggested she ask our guide. Grrrr.

Off we went to lunch. As we were leaving for our next stop, PPG delayed us all while she insisted that the guide wait for her Wi-Fi connection to allow for the transfer of all the photos he took and sent to her. Thankfully, he told her we must go, and the photos would finish transferring when she had Wi-Fi again. Yay, guide, for keeping us moving.

Last moment of "Are you kidding me?" As we were getting into the water to snorkel with stingrays and sharks, we all expressed our desire to purchase the $10 videos. Our guide did a fabulous job using his GoPro and getting individual shots of us underwater. When we got out of the water and were sharing our amazement with each other, we each handed the guide the $10 and our WhatsApp numbers so he could send us our individual footage. Everybody, that is, except PPG. She claimed she didn't have enough money. I snidely asked about our special trip to the ATM. She replied that she didn't think she'd want the videos, but now she does, blah, blah, blah. She got her videos at no charge, while the rest of us paid the required amount. I know it was only $10, but it's the principle of the matter.

I really hate to see bad behavior being rewarded, but I needed to not let her spoil my fabulous snorkel experience.

I tried to stay away from her the best I could and hang out with the other members of our group.

So now you know my pet peeves!

I Dropped My Phone in The Ocean

In general, I am a very careful person and try to always be prepared. Well, I had one of those split-second, bad decision moments when I met an octopus fisherman. We were on the beach across the street from my hotel in Hulhumale, standing in about one foot of seawater and chatting about octopus fishing while he was rinsing out his goggles. How cool was that?

Not wishing to detain him longer than those quick few questions, I asked if it was okay to take a selfie together so I could tell his story later. He agreed, so I juggled my flip-flops, bag of shells, and phone to prepare for our photo. You guessed it… my phone fell into the water. Saltwater. It landed in the sand at the bottom. It was there only as long as it took me to say a bad word and grab it. I know phones are made to be waterproof with limits of time, depth, and conditions, so I hoped I would be lucky since I managed to grab it quickly.

I wiped my phone off on my shirt, took a selfie with the octopus fisherman, and got back to my hotel room as fast as I could. I crossed my fingers and promised not to be so careless ever again as I removed my phone from its protective case. Surprisingly, my phone appeared to still be working. I used a soft towel to completely dry it and even blew on the speaker and USB areas. My dad later suggested using the hairdryer as well. Thanks, Pop. I left the phone out of the case for several hours to make sure it was dry. I totally forgot about the trick where you put your phone in a bag of dry rice for a few days. I Googled the specs for my specific phone, and it looked like it was going to be alright. I breathed a sigh of relief.

I thought everything was okay until the next day when I tried to plug the battery pack into the USB port. I received a warning blast and an announcement to immediately re-move the plug because there might be moisture or debris in the port. (You mean like salt or sand?) How the heck would I charge my phone? The announcement suggested that I charge my phone wirelessly. Luckily, I was traveling with my charging pad. All was well again, or so I thought.

The next day, I tried to transfer the photos from my un-derwater camera's SD card to my phone via memory stick. My phone would not acknowledge the stick the way it had before I dropped it into the ocean. Oh no! Fortunately, the friendly hotel staff took my memory stick and sent my pics to me on WhatsApp. This last issue was enough to finally convince me that something was wrong with my phone.

The next day, I set out to find a phone repair shop. Upon evaluation, the repairman informed me that the USB port was shot and would need to be replaced. It happened to be my lucky day! For $40, he took my phone apart, replaced the port, and ran diagnostics on it to make sure it would work.

You've never seen someone walk as fast as I did to get back to my hotel to test out my memory stick and ensure my phone was repaired! My phone holds my important documents and is my connection to home while I am so far away, so it is extremely important to me.

Yes, it was as good as new! I did a happy dance around my hotel room! Thank you, thank you, thank you!

Philippines

The Philippines, situated in Southeast Asia in the Pacific Ocean, is a vibrant archipelago comprising over 7,600 islands, with 2,000 of them inhabited. The capital city, Manila, is located on Luzon, the largest island. Known as "Asia's Pearl of the Orient," the Philippines boasts a rich culture and stunning landscapes.

The country's name honors Philip II, the King of Spain during the Spanish colonization, which lasted for 333 years. This was followed by 48 years of U.S. tutelage. The Spanish influence is palpable, although Filipino and English are the official languages, with Spanish also spoken.

Governance in the Philippines includes a president and vice-president, with the president elected by the people for a six-year term without the possibility of re-election. Driving is on the right, and the currency is the Philippine peso (PHP), with an exchange rate of $1.00 = 55 PHP. Christianity is practiced by ninety percent of the population.

Two of my favorite Filipino foods are lechon, a delicious

roasted pork dish, and halo-halo (mix-mix), a cold dessert made with ice cream and various sweets. Drinks often come with a plastic seal on top, and meals frequently include a giant spoon instead of a knife. Orders of lechon usually come with thin plastic gloves for tearing apart the pork.

Filipino hospitality is renowned. It is common for clerks or waiters to repeat your order and confirm the amount you paid, for example, "Ma'am, I received 200 pesos from you." This makes transactions straightforward and ensures accuracy.

Navigating the Philippines was a breeze, thanks to the friendly people and the widespread use of English. The food suited my taste perfectly, and I encountered many Americans vacationing or residing here. I am certain I will return!

Whale Sharks: A Bucket List Dream

Many years ago, Steve, a friend of mine, showed me his pictures of scuba diving with whale sharks in the Philippines. I put it on my bucket list to snorkel with them if I ever made it to the Philippines. Well, here I am!

When I was booking this five-month adventure, I only booked air and accommodations for the 17 Islands. I didn't book excursions because I didn't want to be locked into any commitments as I explored. Except for this one! I was so excited about this opportunity that I booked my Oslob Swim with Whale Sharks adventure seven months ago!

When traveling solo, you are asked if you want to be a "joiner" or have a private tour. The advantage of being a "joiner" is that it is less expensive, and you get to make new friends. On this trip, I chose to join a group because it was cost-effective and an excellent chance to meet fellow travelers. There were about a dozen of us, and it was interesting to see the mix of excitement and nervousness on their faces.

We had a 2:00 am start because of the long drive and the need to wait in a very long line to be given a boat number. After all the hullabaloo, we put on our life jackets and loaded into a very narrow wooden boat with outriggers. There were about 30-40 boats in a giant circle around the area where the whale sharks were hanging out. A couple of boats out in the middle were regularly throwing food in the water to keep the whale sharks interested and close for our viewing.

When it was our turn to go into the water, our guides handed us each some goggles. I asked them about a snorkel tube. "No tube, just goggles," they said. How the heck am I supposed to look at whale sharks with my face in the water and giant waves throwing me about if I can't breathe? Oi.

I gave it a go! Trying to calm down after the initial freakout, here's what I saw: beautiful, gentle giants covered in polka dots, gliding effortlessly through the water! I was close enough to touch them, but I didn't. We were instructed not to touch the whale sharks because they are covered in a mucus-like substance that protects them, and being touched could make them vulnerable to infections and harm. Although they were around 15 feet long, I had imagined they would be much bigger. Their very wide mouths were opening and closing around lots of food being filtered through their gill plates. It almost looked like the whales were smiling! The joy I felt at finally seeing these magnificent creatures up close was indescribable.

All I can say is wow! Bucket list...check!

Three Rides, One Adventure: Jeepneys, Tricycles, and Habal Habals

As part of my desire to experience the local traditions and daily ways of life in the Philippines, I decided to try the different modes of transportation. I asked the hotel staff for assistance on how to book a ride to the beach via a jeepney, habal habal, and tricycle. They helped me understand how and where to catch each one. Off I went!

First, I stood in front of my hotel looking for a jeepney. A jeepney is an old, open-air, short bus painted in bright colors with two bench seats running lengthwise. Passengers enter from the back and pass the fee of 13 pesos (23 cents) person by person to the driver. When I saw my first one and tried flagging it down, it passed by me without stopping. I looked at the security guard and asked what I did wrong. "Nothing, ma'am, it was full." Okay, I tried again, and it worked. Jeepneys only service set areas, so my driver dropped me off at his boundary (the church) and yelled out the window for a habal habal driver to take me to Pier 3. Thanks!

Next came the habal habal, which is a motorbike taxi. Helmets are mandatory in the Philippines, so I was given a generic helmet and hopped on the back of the motorbike.

Many people ride motorbikes here because they are cheap, use less gas, are smaller for parking, and can zip in and out of traffic easily. And zip we did. I kept my body tucked tight as we narrowly made our way through traffic from the church to the ferry. Crazy, but I felt totally safe.

I paid 70 pesos ($1.25) for a round-trip ferry ride to Moctan Island. The ferries run every 30 minutes, so there was little wait time before boarding. It was a short trip, just long enough to enjoy a bag of chicharron (pork rinds) sold by a roaming vendor.

My third mode of transportation was the tricycle. As I disembarked the ferry, I saw a row of tricycle taxis. I approached the first one and negotiated a price to the beach. A tricycle is a motorbike taxi with a sidecar attached. Imagine a tuk-tuk with the motorbike on the side instead of front and center. Tricycles are not allowed on busy highways but are very common in smaller towns. My ride was bumpy, but I loved being able to look out without windows blocking the airflow. I asked the driver how many people fit inside a tricycle. One person sits sideways behind the driver on the motorbike, and four sit inside the sidecar—two by two facing each other. Tight squeeze! I sat on the bench seat and saw two tiny, cushioned pads in front of me. I thought they were footrests, but no, those were seats for the other two passengers. Oh my!

I loved experiencing all three local modes of transportation!

Missing My Washer and Dryer

When I began packing for this five-month adventure, I tried to choose clothing that I liked, could be interchangeable, and would quickly dry after washing. Except for my jeans and T-shirt taking two days to dry, everything worked out great.

I fell into a steady groove of soaking my clothes for the day in a sink full of soapy water while I took my shower at night. Then, when my shower was finished, I'd take my soapy clothes and rinse them out under the showerhead. Toweling off and hanging my clothes to dry around the room finished the laundry process for the day. I was lucky enough to have a balcony and drying rack in a couple of my accommodations.

Great system, right? I'm not sure what it is about hand washing in the sink—maybe the lack of soaking time or agitation—but my clothes just never smell as fresh as they do when they've been machine washed. And I'm not sure why I miss my dryer so much, but wearing crunchy clothes and waiting for things to dry are a test of my patience.

Who knows? Maybe I will have a different perspective once I get home and start complaining about doing laundry. Oh, the little things we take for granted…

Where's the Rest of the Silverware?

The first time I ordered a meal in the Philippines (room service), I was given a fork and a large spoon. Too lazy to call downstairs and wait for a knife, I made do. The second time it happened, I realized it wasn't just an oversight.

I began to watch other diners. They used their spoons to tear and cut the food the same way I would use a knife, but they could also use the spoon for scooping. Alright, I thought, I can eat this way too. It grew on me, and I found I didn't really miss my knife that much anymore.

One exception was trying to get the butter out of those teeny tiny butter containers to butter my toast. A giant spoon really doesn't work for that. However, if you turn the spoon around, the handle works like a knife for getting into the corners of the tiny tub.

Just as I figured out one style of eating, I discovered there were other traditional ways to eat. When I was served lechon (chunks of roasted pork), I didn't even get the fork and giant spoon! They placed a tissue box filled with plastic gloves on the table near me. Oh my, the learning curve continues...

Seashells and Prawns: A Day on Caohagan Island

One day, I was on a quest for the perfect beach using local Filipino transportation but ended up disappointed with the local beach choices. They were crowded, noisy, and the water wasn't clear. There was no room to just walk and pick up seashells. I asked the locals where I could find such a beach, and they all told me I needed to take an outrigger boat to Caohagan Island.

Caohagan Island is a small gem in the Philippines. Known for its pristine beaches, crystal-clear waters, and vibrant marine life, it's a paradise for shell collectors and snorkeling enthusiasts. The island is so small that it would only take about an hour to walk around its entire coastline.

In my search for an outrigger boat, I learned that I was too late. All the group tour boats had finished for the day. When someone tells me no, I usually just go ask someone else. Bingo! Guides started coming out of the woodwork, offering a private boat ride to the island. Prices were negotiated, and for 2000 pesos ($36), I hired a captain, a first mate, and an entire outrigger boat! What a bargain!

We set off, just the three of us. Part of me felt like a princess with a giant boat to myself, and another part of me felt wasteful for having such an extravagance. Then I remembered it was only $36, and it was extra income for these two men that they wouldn't otherwise have earned that day because all the tours were over. (Plus, I tipped them an extra 1000 pesos to split for a job well done.) Anyway, I got over it and thoroughly enjoyed myself.

Once on Caohagan Island, I started finding the most beautiful seashells! I couldn't believe my luck! As I was collecting, I stopped to talk to a sea urchin fisherman, a conch fisherman, and a prawn fisherman. The prawn fisherman allowed me to take photos and tried to sell me some of his fresh prawns. I asked him if there was a restaurant on the island where I could eat them. No, but he invited me to his home, and he would cook them for me. I giggled and politely declined.

Later, as I was relaxing and reading my Kindle, he approached me again about purchasing some of his prawns to take back and cook at my hotel. We ended up with a compromise: for a negotiated fair price, he would cook the prawns and rice and bring them to me at the picnic table area. Deal!

OMG, the prawns and garlic sauce were amazing! I don't know if it was the secret spices in his sauce, the fact that those very prawns had just come from the ocean, or the circumstances of how the entire beautiful day evolved, but that was a magical "prawn delight."

Filipino Charmers: Embracing Flirtatious Encounters

When I landed in Cebu, Philippines, I hired a driver to take me to my hotel. He put my luggage in the trunk and gave me the choice of where to sit, so I hopped in the front with him. I was chatting away with him and asking questions about the Philippines. He kept looking over at me, and finally he said he liked my face. I smiled at the compliment and told him it was because I'm a happy person. He very seriously said, "No, it's because you're beautiful."

I knew then that this was going to be a self-esteem-building country. Other experiences followed daily. Another driver asked if I would consider dating a much younger Filipino man (him)? Another guy asked if he could cook for me in his home.

It was very common for my male drivers, guides, or just random people to ask about my age and husband or boyfriend. Once they found out I was single, they tried to match me up with all kinds of cousins and friends who would love to meet me. I just smiled and said I was fine but thank you. I always felt completely at ease and took the compliments in a lighthearted way, never once worried about being alone with a stranger.

Other tourists reported having the same experience. I decided that this was an island of flirts! The Philippines certainly was good for my older woman ego!

The Floating Restaurant Experience

Another unique tour was of the Loboc River, a serene waterway winding through the heart of Bohol. About fifty travelers from different parts of the world boarded a very large open-air barge. Tables lined the edges to capture scenic views, and a beautiful buffet table ran down the center, transforming a working barge into a lovely floating restaurant.

What a fun way to enjoy lunch! We started cruising lazily down the river while a three-member band played local music for us. The food on the buffet was delicious!

The Loboc River is known for its clear emerald waters and lush greenery along its banks. The riverbanks are dotted with nipa palm trees and other tropical vegetation, creating a picturesque backdrop for our journey. As we cruised along, we encountered many other restaurants where people were enjoying their own buffet lunches. We also saw many local children splashing in the river and having a great time. Some teenagers were swinging from ropes tied to tree branches and launching themselves right next to our boat. I think they were showing off, and we all cheered them on.

At one point, our barge stopped next to a floating stage, where we enjoyed local music and dancing. I especially liked the Tinikling dance, where bamboo sticks were clicked together, and the costumed dancers moved between the sticks without tripping on them. I would have made a mess of that and ended up with bloody ankles!

What a unique way to enjoy lunch in the Philippines!

From Cheesy to Magical: My 10,000 Roses Visit

I was traveling back from a very full day in the north of Cebu when I saw a flyer in the backseat of my taxi for 10,000 Roses. My driver said it was beautiful at sunset, so we negotiated the additional cost, and off we went to see 10,000 Roses.

When we arrived in Cordova, my first reaction was, "Oh no, this is going to be cheesy." The perfectly arranged artificial roses in neat rows and the somewhat touristy setup gave me the impression that it might be a tacky attraction. But I had already committed, so what the heck, I gave it a go. I'm super glad I did!

According to an Internet search, the number 10,000 came from ten, meaning perfect, times 1,000. The 10,000 Roses Café & More is an art installation created by a Korean artist, which features ten thousand white LED-powered artificial roses. The roses are planted in a large open area, designed to resemble a field of blooming flowers. Despite being artificial, the roses are actually pretty, especially at dusk when they begin to light up.

We arrived with perfect timing just as the sun was setting. There was a cool deck where you could plop down in a beanbag chair and just "be." After sunset, the roses were all lit with alternating colors pulsing through the garden. Again, it sounds cheesy, but it really was quite magical.

I took advantage of the standard photo ops, then set out for the café, where I enjoyed a chocolate muffin with vanilla ice cream on top that was out of this world. It was the perfect end to an unexpectedly delightful evening.

Sometimes I can't believe my good luck at finding such cool, unexpected things on my travels. I am blessed...

Meeting "The Poverty Fighter"

My brother Bryan, who lives in Oklahoma, has often spoken about a Filipino friend of his named Sal, who is known as "The Poverty Fighter." Bryan and I had even discussed possibly going to the Philippines someday to meet up with Sal and explore the country. We never got around to taking that trip, so when my *Island-Hopping Adventure* included the Philippines, I had to seize this wonderful opportunity to meet my brother's friend.

Despite our busy schedules, Sal made a huge effort to meet me in my hotel lobby so we could chat face-to-face. He even brought two of his students along. What a dynamo! I thought I had a lot of energy, but Sal is me times ten when it comes to energy and vision. Listening to his stories about creating Arapal Nature Farm, a sustainable agriculture community in Cebu that helps uplift the local population through various livelihood programs, was truly inspiring. The farm promotes self-sufficiency by teaching organic farming techniques, producing goat milk, and making coconut oil. Additionally, Arapal Nature Farm emphasizes education by offering student-led tours and maintaining an on-site classroom. The farm also has a strong religious foundation, with a church on the property that serves as a community gathering place. Sal passionately talked about "Trade Not Aid" and promoting "Self-Sustainability Not Dependency."

After our brief visit, the two students, the driver, and I embarked on a three-hour drive north to the farm for the student-led tour.

Upon arrival, I was greeted by the friendliest group of people! We shared a delicious, organic lunch in their gazebo. All the food was grown right there on the farm. Then, it was time to choose my western wear for the tour!

Arapal Farm has a rack of cowboy hats and boots for its guests to wear for an authentic farm feeling while touring. All the guides wore hats and boots, and some even sported bandanas. I chose yellow boots and a yellow cowboy hat! Yeehaw!

The six students had the day off from their online classes to share their knowledge of how everything worked on the farm. They showed me how goat milk is pasteurized, coconut oil is produced, and organic fertilizer is made. I also visited the duck farm, chicken farm, vegetable garden, and water filtration system. The property also includes a classroom, church, guesthouse, dorms, and offices. What a tour! The students did a fantastic job.

I was very grateful for the time everyone put into welcoming and teaching me. Kudos to Sal for all his great work! Sal is not only famous here in the Philippines but also in Texas and Oklahoma. His numerous speaking engagements and partnerships with various churches and organizations in those states have made him well-known there. When I posted about Arapal on Facebook, a handful of people responded, saying, "Oh, I know Sal!" Small world.

Lechon 101: The Perfect Way to Enjoy Roasted Pig

On the previous several islands, I ate a lot of curry and chicken. I am not a fan of curry, I'm sad to say. When I arrived in the Philippines, I was delighted to learn that pork is a popular choice here. Yippee! Lechon (roasted pig) stands out as a local favorite. It is considered both a specialty and a delicacy because it is a traditional dish often prepared for special occasions and celebrations, and it is highly prized for its unique flavor and preparation method. The farm-raised pig is slowly roasted over a charcoal pit, often taking several hours to achieve the perfect crispy skin.

When you order lechon at a roadside cafe, you ask for it by weight in kilos. For instance, I found that one-quarter kilo was more than enough for me. Plus, it usually comes with rice and atchara, which is pickled papaya. You will also be given a clear, lightweight glove.

To mix the dipping sauce for your lechon, combine soy sauce, vinegar, and calamansi (Philippine lime). The ingredients are provided on the table for you to combine yourself. Use your gloved hand to tear apart the bits of pork. Dip them into the sauce you just mixed, close your eyes, and savor this delicious combination! To really top it off, take a bite of the crunchy pork skin served with it. Yum!

You must try lechon while visiting the Philippines, but I will warn you—the ENTIRE roasted pig, head included, is sitting on the counter being carved for your dining pleasure!

Lechon is more than just a meal; it's an experience that captures the essence of Filipino cuisine and hospitality. Enjoying it at a local cafe, surrounded by the vibrant culture of the Philippines, makes it a truly unforgettable treat!

Millions of Sardines: The Dance of the Ocean

One of the popular tours in this part of the Philippines is called the Moalboal Sardine Run. Of course, I couldn't miss out on it! I booked the group tour as a "joiner" and paid online through the GetYourGuide app.

After a hotel pickup, the driver picked up another couple, making our joiner group a total of three. Then we embarked on the long ride to Moalboal. Once we arrived, we rented GoPros, paid a small extra fee for flippers, and selected our life jackets and snorkels. We followed our guide to the beach—no boat needed for this snorkel tour, just straight into the ocean.

We backed into the ocean wearing our flippers. This is a

common technique because walking forward in flippers is awkward and difficult, as the long fins tend to catch on the sand and make you trip. By walking backward, it's much easier to navigate into deeper water without stumbling.

One of our three guides tied all our flip-flops onto a life ring that would float along with us. This was a clever idea because we would be swimming far away from our starting spot, and the current would carry us down the beach. By keeping our flip-flops with us, we would have our shoes when we got out of the water at the end of the tour, no matter how far we drifted.

We put on our snorkel gear and attempted to see this amazing sight of millions of sardines. I was disappointed to discover the water was very cloudy, and the sardines were far below. Great, I wasted my money!

And then…the guides said we had to dive deeply to reach the clearer water. I am not a confident swimmer and didn't want to part with my life jacket. Neither did another girl in our group. The guides do this every day, several times a day, so they understood. "No problem, we push you down!" What?

I'm kind of glad I didn't go first. Watching the process of the other two guests allowed me to realize they didn't die, so I would be okay too.

Here's the process:

1. One guide dives down to the ocean floor with the rented GoPro.

2. Still wearing my life jacket and goggles, I remove my snorkel, get my brave on, and take a deep breath.

3. On the count of three, the other two guides push hard on me so I can be in the middle of the clear water 20 feet below and view this magical scene.

The feeling of being pushed through millions of glittery, dancing sardines was absolutely amazing. The fish dispersed as I entered their masses, shimmering and sparkling as they moved around me. It was like being in the middle of a living, breathing underwater galaxy.

How in the heck the guides knew when to let me up for air, I don't know, but it was always in a timely fashion. After seeing this otherworldly scene, I was so exhilarated that when they asked if I wanted to do it again, the answer was YES, YES, YES!

What an absolute treat! To think I was just telling myself what a waste of money this tour was. Moral of the story: Finish the tour before you judge its value.

Taiwan

Taiwan is an island in East Asia, located in the Pacific Ocean, north of the Philippines and southwest of Japan. The capital is Taipei, where I spent seven days exploring its bustling cityscape, as it is the largest city in Taiwan. Taiwan's history is marked by periods of colonization by the Dutch, Spanish, Chinese, and Japanese. While China claims Taiwan as a province (PRC), Taiwan asserts its independence as the Republic of China (ROC), which can be a bit confusing. The people here are referred to as Taiwanese.

Mandarin is the official language, and about one-third of the population speaks English as a second language. This presented challenges for me when asking questions, ordering food, and reading signs because I know zero Mandarin.

The island is 90 miles wide and 245 miles long from north to south. Taiwan is densely populated with approximately 24 million people. The two main religions are Buddhism and Taoism. The government is led by a president and vice-president, who are elected by the people every four years.

The currency is the New Taiwan Dollar, with $1.00 US equaling 32 TWD. Taiwan's main sources of income include the exportation of steel, electronics, machinery, and chemicals. It is the world's largest supplier of computer chips. The country experienced an economic growth spurt called the "Taiwan Miracle" in the late 1990s. Along with Singapore, Hong Kong, and South Korea, Taiwan is one of the "Four Tigers."

Taiwan ranks highly in terms of civil liberties and has an excellent healthcare system.

During my seven days here, I marveled at the range of experiences I had. I visited the night markets, temples, and even lit a sky lantern in the traditional fashion. I also visited multi-storied shopping malls with stores like Tiffany, Gucci, Versace, Armani, Cartier, Rolex, and Dior. Night markets fit my budget better, but I was happy to see the range of diversity in this country.

My main takeaway from Taiwan was its level of efficiency. Everything was clean, I felt totally safe everywhere, even at night, and everything seemed orderly. The METRO subway/train system was one of the best I've ever used! It was user-friendly for people like me who get lost easily. Taiwan didn't give off warm, cuddly vibes like some of the other countries I've visited. Maybe it was the language barrier or the rain that didn't allow for lingering chats with locals. I'm not sure, but I will say it is an efficient and safe country to visit!

What the Heck Does That Say?

When I arrived in Taipei City and walked into my apartment, the very first thing I noticed was the washing machine. You have no idea how excited I was about the prospect of clean clothes. I divided my dirty clothes into two piles and loaded the first set into the small front-loading machine. I located the laundry detergent under the sink and put my reading glasses on to choose a wash cycle. Oh no!

To my horror, all the settings were in Chinese with no pictures! I had been so excited to FINALLY have clean clothes, but now I was feeling a mix of disappointment and frustration because I couldn't work the machine.

At this point, I didn't know about the Google Translate app I could put on my phone to translate written signs. I messaged my Airbnb host for a quick tutorial for the washer/dryer. Within minutes, she sent me pictures with the translated words on them. What a lifesaver!

Now, I have clean clothes. Thank you!

Launching A Sky Lantern

This was amazing! Our tour group left Taipei City and stopped in Shifen on Old Street. Shifen is a charming town in Taiwan, renowned for its picturesque Old Street that runs alongside active railway tracks. This bustling area is lined with quaint shops and cafes, offering a unique blend of traditional and modern experiences, making it a popular spot for both locals and tourists. Our guide dropped us off at a shop that sold sky lanterns to follow the steps given by the shopkeeper.

First, you must choose a four-colored paper lantern based on your top priorities: health, wealth, marriage, promotion, happiness, popularity, success, etc. The store clerk hangs the three-foot-tall paper lantern on a rack and gives you a set of brushes and black paint. The lantern starts off flat, with four panels that fold out to form a square shape when opened. You paint words on each of the four panels, with the clerk turning the flat lantern as you finish each panel. The words painted on each panel are supposed to fit the goal of the color (for example, the red side should have health wishes, yellow for wealth goals, and pink for happiness).

Well, clearly, I didn't get the memo because I just started painting random words on the first side they hung up for me! When she flipped it to another side, I looked at her funny because I thought I was finished. She pointed at the color chart for me to write my goals based on color. Oh well, I hope that doesn't change my luck because I didn't follow directions.

Once all four sides were completed, a guide took me and my lantern out to the railroad tracks where others were launching their lanterns. He lit the papers hooked onto the cross wires at the bottom of my lantern with a small fire. The lanterns are often made of biodegradable materials like rice paper and bamboo, which will eventually break down once they land. He asked me for my phone camera. I held my lantern ready for this rainy-day launch. My photographer gave me commands for posing while holding my lantern and launching it. Here were some of the poses he requested for my photographs: "cheese, peace, hello, happy, sexy, kitten." I don't remember the rest because I was laughing so hard at "kitten pose."

Once the photo shoot was finished, I took my hands off my sky lantern and watched my written dreams slowly lift off, powered by the flames. My face lit up, and my smile covered my face as my paper lantern slowly disappeared into the heavens. That was pretty darn cool!

Nature's Sculptures at Yehliu

The rock formations at Yehliu Geopark were incredible! There are 180 hoodoo stones at this famous UNESCO site, covering 1700 square meters. Hoodoo stones are tall, thin spires of rock that protrude from the ground. These magnificent formations were created by wind and giant crashing ocean waves over a period of 4,000 years.

Boardwalks covered the slippery areas, while other parts allowed us to walk freely among these naturally created statues. Most of them were twice my height! It felt like I was walking through an obstacle course on Mars.

The nearby ocean waves were fierce, with signs everywhere warning us to be aware of crashing waves. Red lines painted on the ground served as boundaries to keep people safe. One of the coolest parts was the little pools of seawater around these stones, filled with many sand dollars washed in among the rocks.

The unique mushroom rocks had some very creative names, such as the famous "Queen's Head," "Beehive," "Sea Candles," and one of my favorites, "Fairy Shoe."

These geological curiosities were other-worldly!

Dodging a Near Disaster

As previously mentioned, I was grateful to have a washer/dryer combo in my Taipei City apartment. After a wet and muddy day of touring (and not having perfect aim when using Taiwanese floor toilets), my jeans and tennis shoes needed to be thoroughly washed.

I threw these few items into the tiny washing machine, loaded the detergent, and pressed start. I took a quick five-minute shower (limited to the size of the small water heater over the toilet) and came out of the bathroom to a huge surprise!

Apparently, the tennis shoes had banged the door of the washing machine open during the agitation cycle. There were suds and pools of water all over the kitchen floor, and the washing machine was still going, pulsing more suds and water out onto the floor of my 10th-floor apartment! Holy moly! All I could think of was the Brady Bunch episode when the kids used too much soap and filled the laundry room with suds!

As fast as I could, after a few expletives, I ditched the towel I was wearing and used the spare towel to stop the water from potentially finding a way to exit to the floor below me.

Man, I'm glad nobody was traveling with me to witness that mess. It was not pretty.

After the cleanup, I continued the wash cycle while keeping a close eye on the door of the machine. Thirty minutes later, I was grateful to have clean shoes and jeans and to be able to laugh about it!

Hey, I also had a clean floor!

Cracked Delicacies: Discovering Taiwanese Tea Eggs

As I travel through new countries, I constantly see new foods to try or to avoid. Stinky tofu...no. Chicken feet...no. Roasted pig...yes. Waffle balls...yes. Tea eggs...not so sure.

I saw crockpots filled with brown liquid and chicken eggs submerged in this liquid. The sign said "Tea Eggs." I shook my head and walked by them twice. The third time I saw them, I asked my local guide, "What exactly is a tea egg?"

A tea egg is basically a hard-boiled chicken egg that's been soaking in tea for an hour. The tea usually has some soy sauce and other spices in it as well. Once the eggs are hard-boiled and before they are put in the tea mixture, the shells are intentionally cracked. This allows the tea mixture to seep into the cracks and create a marbled spider web pattern on the eggs.

Tea eggs are a popular snack here and can be found in convenience stores like Seven-Eleven. I decided it was time to try one! I picked up the tongs next to the crockpot of brown eggs, lifted one out of the warm liquid, and dropped it into a little clear baggie. I paid NT 13, which is about 43 cents US.

I easily peeled the egg and saw the beautiful dark brown lines that looked like cracked glass. I took a bite and liked it. It was a flavorful hard-boiled egg. I'm not sure I will make tea eggs part of my diet once I get home, but I certainly look at them differently now! The moral of this story: don't knock it till you try it!

New Bonds: A Friend of a Friend in Taipei

Before I set out on this *Island-Hopping Adventure,* I brainstormed which islands I'd add to the mix and talked to friends about my trip. Once the trip was solidified, I announced the dates and places I'd chosen. Several friends and relatives shared their experiences and travels with me.

My friend, Carolina, had a childhood friend living in Taiwan. She gave me her friend's contact information, and Maria and I chatted a few times about my upcoming visit to Taiwan. Months later, as I was boarding my plane from the Philippines to Taipei City, I reconnected with Maria. We planned to meet up, and she generously showed me some of her favorite spots around Taipei. We had such a fun afternoon! We enjoyed ourselves so much that we met up two more times during my week in Taiwan for shopping and lunch.

I can't explain how nice it is to be so far from home and still have a connection with home. What a wonderful example of people connecting with people! And now I have a new friend! Thanks, ladies!

The Early Morning Taxi Challenge

I had been successfully using the MRT (Mass Rapid Transit) system around Taipei City. It was fast, safe, clean, and efficient. By far, it was one of the easiest subway systems I had ever used. However, it didn't begin operations until 6:00 a.m., and I needed to be at a meeting point for my excursion at 5:50 a.m., so I had to flag down a taxi.

I started at my hotel at 5:00 a.m. and waved down two taxis that drove past me with customers inside. I continued walking toward the Metro train station and found a dozen taxis lined up in front. I carefully chose a driver and showed him the printed name of my destination in English. He looked at me like a deer in headlights. This is when Google Translate would have come in handy, but I had no Wi-Fi. I started to head toward another taxi when he said, "Wait."

The taxi driver phoned an English-speaking friend. I gave him the address, and he told the driver. This must be a common practice because my taxi from the airport to my hotel five days ago did the same thing. All good. Or so I thought.

There wasn't much traffic because it was so early, so we arrived at the translated address by 5:20. Perfect amount of extra time to get breakfast and find a bathroom before the guide picked us up at 5:50. The only problem was that the taxi driver dropped me off in front of Exit 2 of the bus station section instead of the train station section. I told him it was the wrong spot. He pointed more emphatically. I paid and got out of the taxi very frustrated.

I knew I was somewhere in the general vicinity, so I started wandering around looking for signs and asking other non-English-speaking travelers. Eventually, I found the perfect helper! He knew exactly where I was trying to go and pointed me in the right direction. I even had time for a potty break and a bite to eat.

Thank goodness for helpful people! Now, I need to figure out a better system with Wi-Fi so I can use my phone for Google Maps and Google Translate.

Exploring Manila: My 11-Hour Layover

The airline changed my flight from Taipei, Taiwan to Port Moresby, Papua New Guinea at the last minute, and the new flight included an 11-hour layover in Manila, Philippines. Having enjoyed my previous visit to Cebu, I decided to fill out the necessary documents to leave the airport and explore. The security and customs process was surprisingly smooth. After a quick pass through customs, I was free to go. My carry-on suitcase was checked straight through to my destination, so I didn't need to deal with that. For a tiny fee, I dropped my heavy backpack at a storage locker facility and headed for the information desk.

There were no scheduled excursions from the airport, but I was advised to find a taxi or a "Grab" driver and negotiate a price for the day. Grab is similar to Uber, providing ride-hailing services through a mobile app. And off we went!

My first request was Dolemite Beach. My driver dropped me off, and I told him I'd see him in an hour. Wondering why there were no people on this beautiful white sandy beach, I asked a nearby vendor and discovered it was closed on Thursdays. Guess what day it was? Yep, Thursday.

I spotted a horse and carriage and asked the price for a ride to another beach. We negotiated a price for him to take me, wait 30 minutes, then return me to my driver. "Chocolate," the horse, clip-clopped along to the next beach. I knew I'd been tricked when I saw more trash than beach, and a little naked boy ran out of the water, one hand covering his privates and the other asking me for money. I turned around and got back into the carriage for the return ride.

I need to mention here that Chocolate was a skittish horse. He wore blinders, and his 15-year-old driver hit him with a stick to get him moving. This was turning out to be a sad experience rather than a joyful one. Then it got even worse.

A dog lunged at Chocolate, spooking him so much he fell backward into our cart, twisting it. I thought we were getting dumped! Chocolate recovered, the dog's owner retrieved it, and the carriage driver checked on his horse and bent a side bar back into place. I couldn't wait to get away from the cart and driver!

Ready for this? The cart driver did not take me back to my original driver as promised but basically pointed to where I needed to cross the street to find him. Grrr. Then he had the nerve to ask for a tip "for Chocolate." Boy, did I have to refrain from telling him what to do with his request!

Eventually, I made it back to my driver, and we moved on to Fort Santiago.

At Fort Santiago, I met the "Singing Lady." One section of the old stone ruins was labeled as an amphitheater. To the horror of her two teenage daughters, a mom started belting out "Figaro." Her daughters were embarrassed, while I started clapping! I told her that Figaro was my trail name from when my friend Suzanne and I hiked a small section of the Appalachian Trail many years ago. We came across a bear while hiking, and I had heard that singing opera would scare him away. So, I belted out Figaro at the top of my lungs, and the bear took off running. It worked. Now the lady and I had a connection about frightening animals and people with Figaro!

The last stop was SM by the Bay Amusement Park, an entertainment complex located by Manila Bay and part of the SM chain of shopping malls. It ended up being my favorite. I took a spin on the giant Eye Ferris Wheel to have a look around. Then, I walked the boardwalk and watched the glorious sunset over the bay alongside many local people. I sampled the "fair foods," took photos, and generally just enjoyed people-watching. What a fantastic way to end a day that started off not so great.

My driver returned me to the airport so I could catch my connecting flight. What a great alternative to sitting in the airport for 11 hours!

Papua New Guinea

I must say this is the only country I've been nervous about visiting. I registered with the embassies in each country before I left the United States and received about half a dozen alerts regarding riots or possible dangers there. Not a good start.

Papua New Guinea is correctly pronounced pah-poo-uh new ginney. I know this because I'd been saying it wrong all along. I finally asked my guide, and he helped me with that. Most people just call it PNG.

PNG is made up of about 600 islands. The main island, New Guinea, is the second largest island in the world and is shared with Indonesia. The country of Papua New Guinea occupies the eastern half of this island, as well as numerous smaller islands. It is in the region of Oceania in the Pacific and is just north of Australia. The population is over 17,000,000. The capital is Port Moresby. Driving is on the left. PNG has a prime minister, not a president. PNG is one of the ten poorest countries in the world. Their currency is the Papua New Guinea Kina. One United States dollar equals 3.76 PNG Kina. PNG has been ruled by Germany, Great Britain, and Australia. It gained its independence in 1975, though Australia still sends millions of dollars in aid annually.

PNG is the most linguistically diverse country in the world, with 850 known languages. English is one of the main languages used. My guides and drivers tried to teach me words and phrases in Pidgin. I failed miserably, but they got a kick out of my attempts!

There are at least 600 tribes living in PNG. Some of the most well-known are the "Mudmen" of the Asaro tribe and the "Crocodile Men" of the Chambri tribe. The Mudmen wear masks made of mud, and the Crocodile Men use skin scars to resemble the scales of a crocodile. These scars are created through a painful process of cutting and healing, often as part of a rite of passage into manhood. In recent years, more than 40 uncontacted tribes have been identified. They live in the rainforest of West Papua.

Christianity is the largest religion here, with 95.6% of the population adhering to it. There are many different branches of Christianity due to the activity of missionaries from different churches. I chatted with a group of missionaries while sitting at the airport one day. Many indigenous practices and superstitions remain. Some still believe that certain people are witches.

Many people joked with me about "watching out for cannibals" on my tour of PNG. Once I got to know my driver and felt I could ask him questions, I asked about this. He said that long ago it was a common practice, but now only one tribe still does it, and they only eat people when they're dead. So, I googled it. I learned that open cannibalism had almost entirely ended in the 1950s.

PNG is one of the most rural countries and has many undocumented species of plants and animals. It is known for its United States military bases, amazing scuba diving, extreme wilderness activities, and learning about isolated tribes and their cultures.

I caution anyone going to PNG to be careful due to the high levels of serious crime. There is a police presence, but corruption can be an issue.

Beachside Surprises: Basketball and Rugby at Ela

On my second day in Port Moresby, I hired a guide through the airport visitors' center to stay with me and take me to several places for a set fee. He acted as a driver, guide, and bodyguard for the day! Three for the price of one—what a bargain! I suspect that he also took on the role of a bodyguard because I was a woman traveling solo.

My first requested destination was Ela Beach. I had to leave my flip-flops on because of the litter and broken glass on the beach. I was picking up seashells and enjoying watching the locals splash in the water when I heard a bouncing basketball. Visions of my Denver Nuggets popped into my head as I walked toward the action. With my guide following, I plopped down on the cement wall to watch. There were three courts of grown men, ranging in age from 20 to 40, engaged in informal Saturday games next to the beach. What a treat!

I was still smiling from that unexpected treat when I heard loud shouts, slapping bodies, and a whistle blowing. I asked my guide what was going on. He told me that the guys were practicing drills in the sand for their upcoming rugby match. How cool is that? There was full contact, no pads, sand-flying tackles right in front of me. I sat down and watched that too.

Wow, and I thought I was just going to the beach to pick up shells. That didn't come close to the joy I got from watching these sports on the beach. Sometimes, the unplanned things turn out to be the best things!

Up Close with Playful Tree Kangaroos

I am an animal lover! When traveling to a new country, I try to learn about the animals endemic to that region and then go see them or interact with them if possible. While in Papua New Guinea, the tree kangaroo captivated my attention.

Tree kangaroos are found in Australia, Indonesia, and Papua New Guinea. Of the world's 14 species, 12 are found in New Guinea, with eight of those in Papua New Guinea. They are mammals and a bit of a mixture between a lemur and a kangaroo. They have short hind legs, strong forelimbs, hooked claws for climbing, and a long tail. The tail doesn't wrap around tree limbs but is used for balance and helping the tree kangaroo launch itself for a big jump! They eat leaves, moss, flowers, and tree bark.

I discovered that the best place to see them was Port Moresby Nature Park. Off I went! What a great experience it was. I was so afraid I would be viewing them in cages and not get to see them up close. Absolutely not!

In this nature park, there are different species of tree kangaroos, and they are sectioned off in giant enclosed walk-through areas like an aviary. There are two separate doors for entering and exiting each section to prevent a crafty critter from tailgating out with a guest. The metal walkway is up in the air, so I feel like I am walking through the treetops with them. What a great way to give guests an in-person experience.

My favorite part of this tree kangaroo experience came when I entered a section with two playful reddish-tan tree kangaroos. They were so perfect they looked like fake stuffed animals! They weren't sleeping in the trees like the others but were moving around. When I entered, they stared at me. As I slowly approached, they hopped up on the rail and stared at me some more. I was very still and talking in a quiet voice like I would speak to a dog or cat. They were certainly interested in this non-threatening human just hanging out with them. I didn't try to touch them, even though they were close enough I could have. After a while, they got used to me, then...ready for this? They started chasing each other and grabbing each other's tails like they were kittens! I got to witness them using their jumping and climbing skills during play. What a special treat!

So Many Snakes!

I was warned about many things when I announced that Papua New Guinea was on my list of 17 islands, but the danger of snakes was not one of them. It didn't even cross my mind until I visited the Nature Park in Port Moresby.

The reptile section displayed several tree-dwelling and ground-slithering snakes that made my skin crawl. I don't mind snakes in general, but I hate being surprised by them, especially if I need to look up in the trees AND down on the ground!

I learned that there are 112 different species in Papua New Guinea, and eight of them are venomous. That's too many for me! There was also a display board near the snake exhibit, educating people on what to do in case of a snake bite. Yikes!

On the way back to my hotel, I expressed my concern to my driver about possibly encountering a snake on a hike. Are you ready for his response? Hold onto your hats. He matter-of-factly said, "They only bite bad people." I think my mouth fell open. Then I asked, "Won't they bite you if you step on them?" It gets worse... He said, "Maybe, but they won't hurt you if you're a good person." I held my tongue in shock at the misinformation. However, I remained cautious, and it didn't deter me from going on any hikes.

Stained Smiles

As I interacted with people in Port Moresby, I couldn't help but notice a striking feature: a vast majority of them had reddish-orange teeth. While I've seen this in other countries, it seemed particularly prevalent here. Curious, I asked my driver what caused their mouths to turn that color.

He explained that it was due to chewing betelnut—a stimulant. It's prepared by combining a bean-like green called mustard (daka) with lime powder (kambang), turning the mixture orange. As it's chewed, people spit out the reddish-orange juice onto the streets, sidewalks, or grass. It's quite a sight!

Chewing betelnut provides a burst of energy like caffeine or tobacco. Interestingly, many places I visited had signs posted saying "No Betelnut" with fines imposed, although enforcement seemed questionable given the splatters of orange or red stains I saw everywhere.

I also wondered if children were allowed to chew it. Apparently not, but I did spot a few kids with unmistakable orange smiles. It's probably not easy for them to hide that from Mom and Dad!

Friendly Souls in a Tough City

Despite all the warnings about the dangers in Port Moresby, PNG, I found some of the friendliest people at the airport, hotel, and beach.

When I landed and walked outside, a security guard stayed by my side while I waited for my ride. A lady from a different tour company asked which hotel shuttle I was waiting for and called them for me. Everyone smiled and was very helpful.

At my hotel, the staff went above and beyond to be courteous and kind. The security guard provided safety information, and one of the desk clerks loaned me her personal phone charger when I told her the one I brought was incorrect.

The biggest show of friendliness was at the beach. When I smiled and said hello, faces lit up, and greetings were returned. When I asked if I could take photos of people, the answer was always yes, and I was rewarded with thanks when I showed them their photo. The children especially enjoyed it. A father and son even yelled hello at me from the water when they saw me taking photos of other people.

It was refreshing to find this goodness in a city filled with cautions.

Fishing Fun with the Local Kids

My fishing experiences have been very different in each country, and except for my deep-sea charter on Reunion Island, I haven't caught anything worth bragging about. When three different people told me to go fishing at the Adventure Park, my expectations were low.

My guide drove me to the park, and we proceeded to the admissions desk. The cost for fishing in the pond was 20 Kina, and for an extra 5 PKG, they sold me a hand line rig and a bag of tiny hooks. My guide helped me purchase a few scones for bait, and we walked to the pond. Scones are small, slightly sweet, and dense bread-like pastries. I had never used scones for bait before, so this was a novel experience for me. The total cost for everything was $9 US.

As I was flinging the hand line out into the water, then jerking the line and missing the crafty little fish, we gathered a small group of curious boys. They came to the water's edge and watched me land two fish under three inches each. What? I didn't know fish that tiny could get a hook into their mouths.

I asked the boys, ranging in age from 7-12, if they wanted to try, because I wasn't having much luck.

Their faces lit up, and all said "Yes." I showed them how to roll the dough of the scones into tiny balls and put it on the hook. They each took a turn, lost the fish, then went back for more dough over and over.

I got so caught up in watching them try to catch a fish that I didn't even care about fishing anymore. My guide and I cheered them on for about half an hour, then I was ready to move on. I left the hand line rig, extra hooks, and bait with the boys and reminded them to share. (Not sure how that went after I left.)

Today's local fishing experience was more about the locals and less about the fishing! All good.

Staying Safe in a City of Risks

Although I had some wonderful experiences in Papua New Guinea, several incidents gave me chills:

I received multiple text alerts through the STEP site about riots, expected unrest, and anger over fuel shortages in Papua New Guinea. The security officer at the airport cautioned me about traveling solo and strongly suggested that I hire a driver and guide everywhere I went. The security personnel at the hotel all but forbade me to set out on foot alone, repeatedly telling me how unsafe it was.

When I took the free shuttle back to the airport because the promised Wi-Fi at the hotel was down, the clerks at the information desk also warned me not to go anywhere alone. I had two days of sightseeing with a driver who served as my guide and jokingly referred to himself as my bodyguard. I tipped him well for his constant vigilance. I asked him why everyone kept warning me about how dangerous Port Moresby was. He didn't know, but he stayed glued to my side for two days. Thanks for that.

While at the beach, I stopped and chatted with a man from South Africa who'd been living there with his wife and dog for several years. I thought I might get a non-local's opinion on the safety concerns. He said his wife couldn't take the threat of crime anymore, so she moved to Sydney. He was in the process of following her once he completed the procedure for transporting a dog to Australia. I asked him to explain. In a nutshell, many desperate people from local villages moved to the big city to find work. When the jobs were not found, some turned to a life of crime.

I Googled Port Moresby and discovered it is a hotspot for violent criminal behavior, including theft, carjacking, break-

ing and entering, domestic violence, serial assault, and mur-
der. What?

Time to get the heck out of Dodge!

Urgent Escape: From Port Moresby to Paradise

When I was traveling through Antananarivo, Madagascar, I decided the big city with its crime, noise, and pollution
was not for me. I booked a flight and got out of there, and I
was so glad I did. Now, in Port Moresby, Papua New Guinea,
I'm feeling an even stronger urge to leave. Many people have
warned me about the crime here and how unsafe it is, especially for solo travelers. It's time to get outta here!

I spent about three hours researching neighboring countries, other islands within PNG, and even going to my next
destination five days early. Everything was an added, unexpected expense, but I decided I couldn't put a price on safety
and comfort. I booked a flight to the island of New Britain,
which is about the size of New Jersey. There, I planned to stay
at a resort with a private beach, activities, and a restaurant.

I spoke to the manager of my current hotel and asked for a
refund for the four nights I would not be staying with them.
Despite booking directly with them and not through a third
party, the policy was no refunds. Since the room was still
mine and paid for, I left some of my bulkier items there and
headed to the airport. I planned to return the night before
my departure to the next country. I know it sounds like a bit

of backtracking, but I checked the cost and length of flights and layovers before booking this last-minute flight.

I usually take pride in mingling with the locals, but this time, I'm opting for security. There's nothing wrong with going with your gut and changing the plan!

Echoes of the Past: WWII Plane Wrecks

One of the excursions offered from my resort in West New Britain, PNG, was to visit the site of two planes that crash-landed during WWII. I'm not a history buff, but I do like airplanes, and I especially like unique opportunities. Plus, I figured I could learn a few things.

My driver and two resort staff members (in case we got stuck in the mud) loaded me into a four-wheel drive vehicle, and we set out. The drive was scenic and bumpy, with the rugged landscape offering a beautiful backdrop to our journey. When we arrived, I was surprised at how well-trimmed the grass and bushes were around the two planes. The villagers maintain the area, ensuring the planes remain preserved.

We parked on a dirt and grass road, and I could see both wrecks, one on either side of the road on a trail. My guide told me this trail is an old airstrip. The airstrip had originally been built by the Germans for exporting coconut and cocoa when they had control of New Guinea. It was abandoned before the war. The Allied forces used this abandoned airstrip during WWII in their fight against the Japanese. We walked down the trail to the left to visit the first plane wreck.

This plane was an American B-25H Mitchell Bomber. In 1944, it developed engine trouble and crash-landed on this airstrip. All three crew members survived. As I walked around the plane, I envisioned all those movies I watched where actors lost in the forest stumbled upon an old plane crash filled with drugs, skeletons, and snakes! I peered inside and didn't see any of those things, but there were vines and even a tree growing inside.

The second plane was from New Zealand and was an NZ4522 Lockheed Vega Ventura. It crash-landed on this airstrip when a Japanese bullet went through its fuel line. All three of its crew survived as well. I couldn't believe I was touching a part of history from 1944.

These two planes are the last in the world to have the original outfitting of artillery. I asked my guide what kept people from stealing parts or vandalizing the sites. He told me the people of a neighboring village oversee protecting the planes, and in return, they receive a portion of the fees collected from tourists like me.

It was cool to see these planes in such a remote part of the world!

Exploring the World of Palm Oil

As I was flying from Port Moresby to Hoskins on the island of New Britain in Papua New Guinea, I saw thousands and thousands of strategically lined-up palm trees. Everywhere! The pattern from the air looked like a painting, it was so perfect. I knew that would be one of my first questions when I got picked up from the airport.

It turns out there are 21 plantations of oil palms here on the western side of the island. Palm oil is big business here! When the Germans controlled PNG, they imported coconut trees and cocoa for their income. Since then, most of those have been replaced with oil palms because they are much more profitable. Oil palms are an efficient crop and produce high quantities over small areas of land year-round. There's a huge market for palm oil as it is used in about 50% of the packaged products found in supermarkets globally. Palm oil is used in food items such as donuts, pizza, and chocolate. It's also used in toothpaste, shampoo, deodorant, and lipstick.

There are two types of oil that come from these nuts. The outer section produces industrial oil, while the inner kernel can be used for oil in cooking and cosmetics. There are many palm oil mills, kernel crushing mills, and refineries on this island.

My first question was, "Do people climb the trees to harvest them?" No, the cluster of fruits (called bunches) is harvested with an aluminum pole that is 12 meters long. It has a little curved knife on the end. The bunches are cut, and the person below quickly gets out of the way. The bunches can weigh between 10-25 kilos (22-55 pounds) each and have little spiky things between the fruits. Ouch. Each bunch contains many individual bright red-orange fruits. If some of the fruits fall, they are also collected. Nothing goes to waste here.

My next question was, "What happens when you can't reach them with the pole anymore?" They replace the tall trees with new baby trees from the nursery. It takes about nine months for the new tree to start producing fruit. A mature tree can produce 12-14 bunches each year. One ton sells for about $100 US.

Many local people have oil palms on their property and would sell the bundles by the roadside. Trucks would come by, pick them up, and load them into bigger trucks to take to the factories.

What's the big controversy over palm oil? The main problem is that deforestation, in order to plant the palms, is destroying the habitat of some endangered species. Some suggest a switch to other oils, but that would basically shift the problem to other parts of the world and threaten other habitats. Damned if you do, damned if you don't.

Muddy Trails and Lucky Breaks

We were on our way to the Hot River, a natural geothermal stream in Papua New Guinea known for its soothing warm waters and scenic surroundings. The roads, however, were very sketchy, and my driver referred to them as "dusty bumpy." Because there had been a lot of rain lately, I told him he could drop the "dusty" part of that description. Well, we could have totally changed it to "muddy, treacherous."

The visit to the Hot River was spectacular, but on the way back to the resort, it started raining again, which added even more challenges to the one-hour drive. We were in a four-wheel drive vehicle equipped with a snorkel, a special exhaust system that extends above the vehicle's hood, designed for crossing small rivers and deep mud puddles without damaging the engine. This is common for vehicles in this area. My driver also had two staff members with him just in case we got stuck, which we did.

We were trying to go around a parked truck that was loading palm oil nuts. We all felt it when the truck slid and immediately sunk the front right tire all the way to the fender. A few bad words came out of the mouth of the normally professional driver. All four of us climbed out to examine the situation. Not good.

But this was our lucky day because we were right next to a giant palm oil truck! The guys all started scrambling to find ropes and chains. My driver got down and used his hands to dig away the thick mud that had caked around the front tire. The giant truck maneuvered into place. The rain continued to sprinkle down, and nobody seemed to pay any attention to it. My swimsuit and cover-up were still wet from swimming in the Hot River, so I didn't care either.

After trying two chains tied together (nope) and a thin rope (it broke), the men finally doubled the ropes and pulled out our vehicle. A sigh of relief, many thanks, and handshakes closed the matter. Nobody asked for money or expected any. It's just what you do when someone needs help.

As we made our way back to the resort, I reflected on how grateful I was that we got stuck where we did. My mind ran through another scenario where we got stuck in the boonies and night was approaching. There was no cell service this far out in the middle of nowhere. But we had three guys in the truck, they knew the route, and we had a resort full of staff who knew where we were going for our excursion.

All's well that ends well!

Cash Drop: The Money Houses of PNG

Before workers in Papua New Guinea had bank accounts for electronic paycheck deposits, there were money houses. I asked my guide to tell me the story, and here's his version.

There were 21 oil palm plantations in West New Britain, Papua New Guinea. Each plantation had its own group of workers who needed to be paid every two weeks. Workers used to be paid in cash, but it was not safe to deliver large amounts of cash by driving to each plantation due to the threat of robbery.

This is where the money houses came in. Plantation owners built 21 small cinderblock buildings, one for each plantation, each with a large funnel on the roof. Workers from each plantation would arrive at a set delivery time to pick up their wages. Every two weeks, a helicopter would carry 21 bags of workers' wages, flying within one and a half meters of the funnel, and drop the specific bag of cash into the corresponding money house. The plantation owner would then distribute the wages to the workers, and they would be off.

I asked why they couldn't get robbed at the money house. My guide explained that there were too many people and too much security. Pretty clever, if you ask me!

Of Course I'll Give It a Go!

I was standing outside the market with two staff members from my resort and noticed one of them had stained teeth from chewing betelnut. I asked him to show me how he mixes the three ingredients to get the desired effect. He pulled out the betelnut, the mustard pod, and the lime powder in a little container. I snapped a few photos, and some local people started to gather around.

They asked if I wanted to try it. I said yes, just a tiny bit so I could get the flavor without the zing.

First, we had to get inside the green, hard betelnut to reach the seed inside. How do you do this? You bite it to get it started, then peel it. Next, you put the entire nut in your mouth and chew it. I'm curious, but not crazy! I peeled off the tiniest portion possible and chewed it.

Now it was time for the other ingredients. The end of the bean-like mustard is snapped off and dipped into the small container of lime powder (crushed baked shells). They instructed me to bite off the very tip end that had both ingredients on it. At this point, my guide had returned to coach me as well, and a small crowd had gathered to watch the foreigner try betelnut for the first time. There were quite a few chuckles as I made weird facial expressions based on the bitter taste.

Once all three items hit my tongue, my mouth turned bright orange. I opened my mouth for my camera to show me the outcome. Holy cow, and I only had a tiny bit! I was instructed to spit into the gutter filled with rainwater. More laughter, a bit of cheering, and, of course, a selfie with all my PNG onlookers!

Back at the vehicle, my guide told me to rinse my mouth twice before we left and then to brush my teeth once I made it back to my bungalow. I thanked the crew for showing me how to properly partake in one of their daily customs. I also told them their betelnut was safe around me because it was not something I would ever do again. Yuck!

Vanuatu

Vanuatu, a country of 80 islands in the South Pacific Ocean, boasts a unique blend of cultures and natural wonders. The capital city, Port Vila, is the heart of this nation, which has a population of 320,000 people. Christianity is the predominant religion, and the official languages are Pidgin, French, and English.

The islands were first inhabited by Melanesian people. Captain Cook named the islands New Hebrides in 1774. Vanuatu was under the rule of both France and the UK before gaining independence in 1980. In Vanuatu, driving is on the right side of the road. The country has a president elected every five years, and the currency is the Vanuatu vatu, with $1.00 USD equating to 119 VUV.

Vanuatu is renowned for its scuba diving, snorkeling, waterfalls, and active volcanoes. Surprisingly, bungee jumping was invented here! Tanna Island is home to Mount Yasur, the world's most accessible active volcano. Despite its many attractions, Vanuatu remains one of the least visited countries, with only 95,000 visitors annually. For comparison, the similarly sized island nation of Fiji welcomes over 800,000 tourists each year.

The national dish of Vanuatu is Lap Lap, a baked pudding made of yam, banana, and manioc mixed with coconut milk and wrapped in banana leaves. It's baked under hot volcanic stones. Kava is also popular here, with 80 different types available. Known for its relaxing, narcotic properties, kava looks like muddy water. I tried it in Fiji and again in Vanuatu, but I didn't like it in either place.

Living in Vanuatu comes with its hazards, including droughts, floods, earthquakes, tsunamis, and cyclones. It was surprising to learn that cannibalism was practiced here until as late as 1969. Who knew? Maybe that's one reason tourism isn't so great! Hahaha!

Chair in the Air: High Above the Ground

While searching for unique things to do in Vanuatu, I discovered a place that offered a suspension bridge, zipline, canyon swing with a dramatic drop (no thank you), and a brand new "Chair in the Air" (yes, please). I had the tourist office in my hotel make arrangements for that same afternoon.

What the heck is a "Chair in the Air," and why would someone like me, who's afraid of heights, ever want to do that? First, I've never even heard of a chair in the air, so count me in on anything new and strange. Second, the more I do things that challenge my fear of heights, the smaller my fear becomes.

145

The "Chair in the Air" is basically a seat hammock with footrest straps that is reeled out on cables over a seventy-meter-deep canyon. I was strapped into the seat with a harness around my legs and waist, just in case the seat broke. The cables looked sturdy, and I chatted with the Aussie owner while he prepped the equipment.

I had my package of Tim Tams, my all-time favorite Aussie cookie, which I had purchased at the Sydney Airport, and a bottle of water in my lap. As I was slowly and gently reeled out, I decided that looking out at the ocean, the waterfall, and the nearby suspension bridge was probably a good idea. Don't look down!

I sat in the chair enjoying the view for half an hour. I even chatted with some fellow tourists on the suspension bridge. It was relaxing! There was another set of cables right next to mine if two people wanted to enjoy sitting next to each other that far up.

What a cool and different activity! I recommended it to several tourists who asked me what they should do in Port Vila, and I asked them to tell the owner that Yvonne sent them!

Exploring Vanuatu's Unique Underwater Post Office

Among the unusual things to do and see in Vanuatu, the world's only underwater post office made the list! I took the "B" bus to the dock, where the boat takes you, at no charge, to Hideaway Island. I paid the entrance fee for the island and selected my waterproof postcard. I addressed it and wrote a message to my parents in Texas. Then I rented snorkel gear and a noodle and went in search of the underwater post office.

I snorkeled to the first floating platform and looked down, and there it was! Not quite as clean and shiny as the ads showed it, but there it was. It was farther down than I expected because of the high tide. I knew I wouldn't be able to let go of my noodle and snorkel down (maybe 10-12 feet). So, I asked another snorkeler if she would take my postcard down. She tried three times and almost made it but couldn't quite reach it. No worries.

I tucked the postcard inside my swimsuit and set off to enjoy snorkeling nearby. I paddled over to the reef and WOW! The colorful fish were eye-popping! Then a fellow snorkeler mentioned that the snorkeling was even better at the second reef. Curious and excited, I headed off, and WOW, WOW, WOW! The water was crystal clear, and the variety of fish was simply astounding! It was raining the entire time I was snorkeling, but it didn't affect the amount of fun I was having!

When I needed a rest, I headed back to shore and handed my postcard to the local dive master to post for me. He said that the postcards are collected daily and canceled with a special embossing tool showing where they originated. I think my mom and dad will really like this one!

Budget Adventures on the "B" Bus

Getting around on each island while on a budget has been an adventure. Taking a taxi or renting a car is expensive, so learning about the local transportation is one of the first things I do upon arrival. In Vanuatu, that mode is the "B" bus.

What does that mean exactly? There are many tourists in Vanuatu, especially when a 3,600-passenger cruise ship docks once or twice a week. Lots of tour vans are needed to handle the crowds. How do you know which white or silver van/bus is public versus private? The answer is a red capital letter B in front of the license number of a public vehicle. Thus, the name "B" bus.

Stand anywhere you see one and wave to get the driver's attention. If they stop, ask if they can take you to your destination and hand them 150 vatu. Hop in, and it's as simple as that! The driver will pick up and drop off multiple passengers along the way, but you'll get there for just over $1. What a bargain!

But hold on. There's a catch. Sometimes a "B" bus will have passengers that have asked to be dropped at a bar or store and want the driver to wait for them. They paid extra for this courtesy, but the driver is still available to give you a ride after the others are finished with their business and ready to go. Cheap if you have plenty of time.

I also learned that walking a few extra steps at the airport can save you a significant amount of money. At the door of

148

the airport, fares range from 1500-2500 vatu. Savvy travelers know to walk out the door and across the street, hand the driver 150 vatu, and get the same result.

Oh, the little things we learn after spending some time in a different country.

Knock Knock, Prankster Alert

After a long day of snorkeling and mailing a waterproof postcard to my parents, I took a short rest. I then enjoyed a Melanesian BBQ and performance by my hotel pool. Feeling ready for bed, I decided to call it a night and headed up a short flight of stairs to my room.

I was changing into my PJs when there was a knock at my door. "Who is it?" Silence. I resumed getting ready for bed when another knock echoed through the room. "Who's there?" Again, nothing.

Now, slightly paranoid because it was 9:15 p.m. and nobody was saying, "Oh, sorry. Wrong room," I heard a knock again. "Room service." My paranoia spiked. I wedged a chair under the doorknob and found a butcher knife in the kitchen drawer, holding it tightly as my heart pounded.

Knock, knock. "Room service." I yelled through the door, "Go away."

On the final knock, I was on my cell phone near the door, speaking loudly to the reception desk, asking them to send someone to room five to check for the annoying knocker. I requested they not knock on my door, as I WAS NOT OPENING IT for anyone. They called me a few minutes later to inform me that nobody was hanging around, suggesting it was probably a prankster.

I chalked it up to the excessive kava consumption by the pool that night, suspecting someone was going door to door for kicks. No matter what, I built an obstacle course of furniture from my door to my bed before I went to sleep that night. Darn kava!

The Unspoken Rules of Island Loyalty

While visiting Vanuatu, I wanted to fly to the island of Tanna to see the famous active Mount Yasur Volcano. I really wanted to spend the night in a treehouse, which was a popular option for accommodation near the volcano. In the process of booking my flights and accommodations, I also needed to arrange transportation from the airport to the treehouse and the volcano and then back to the airport. My Internet search said that was no problem; I could book a ride from a taxi upon arrival for 1,000 vatu.

I called Jake, the owner of the treehouse, to confirm my reservation. Jake asked if I wanted to book a ride. I asked his price and just about fell out of my chair! His price was 5,000 vatu to the treehouse, then an additional 3,000 up to the parking lot of the volcano. OUCH. I thanked him and told him I was on a budget and would book my own transfer once I arrived. He said, "If you change your mind, I'll be in town and happy to pick you up." Thanks.

Here's where "Island Loyalty" begins. Apparently, everybody knows Jake. Enough key people knew of my plan to thwart the system and get a ride to Jake's treehouse from a cheaper source than Jake.

Upon arrival at the teeny tiny airport in Tanna, one blonde foreigner (me) emerged looking for a ride to The Summit Treehouse. Everyone's response was, "You mean Jake's place?" Yes.

The lady collecting departure taxes yelled to a guy in an orange t-shirt who confirmed that I was THE ONE looking for a ride to Jake's place. His stall tactics went like this: "You want a cheaper ride by sharing with others?" Yes, please. "I have two other people coming, and we can share, but you must wait for them." I checked with him a couple of times, and he let me know they hadn't arrived yet.

Now, I'm getting a bit nervous as all the 40-50 people who were on my plane are leaving, as are all the taxis. This airport is in the boonies, so there are no other options. I asked Mr. Orange Shirt one more time if we were still going as a party of three. He said, "No, they never showed up, but let me ask the guy in the brown truck if he's going to the east side of the island, and you can pay him."

As Mr. Orange Shirt walked away, a guy in a blue shirt approached me and said he was a friend of Jake's. Mr. Orange Shirt was in the brown truck driving away and waving the old "she's all yours now" wave to Mr. Blue Shirt. I told him I thought I had a ride, and he pointed out, "Where? I don't see a guy in an orange shirt, AND all the taxis have left now. Jake said I could pick you up and take you to him

in town for the rate he quoted you on the phone yesterday."
Well, I guess I have no choice; let's go.

Wow, the Internet might be able to tell me the price of a
ride for a local, but it knows NOTHING about the honor
code of friends in the island business.

Scritch, Scratch

My journey to Tanna began with a drive from the airport
straight to the volcano by Jake, the owner of the treehouse
I had booked. Unfortunately, the volcano tour was canceled
due to excessive rain and flooding. We continued to the treehouse. Jake honked to let his wife know we had arrived. A
very robust and happy woman came toward us, carrying an
umbrella and a large light for the treehouse. She introduced
herself as Jake's wife. She then led me up two flights of steep
wooden stairs into the treehouse. I only had my backpack
since this was a quick one-night adventure. She showed me
around and exited with a smile.

The treehouse, built by Jake, seemed very sturdy. I was
happy about that because I was up pretty high. There was a
wooden floor and walls with a tin roof. Multicolored sheets
were nailed to the walls to cover some of the openings to the
outside. I had a choice of two beds, a queen and a single, both
with mosquito netting. There was also a little room off the
back that housed a flushing toilet. I asked about running water, and yes, there was a spigot outside the front door. All set.

It was pouring rain, so even though it was only 6:30 p.m.,
I declined dinner and said I wanted to go to sleep. Our vol-

cano tour had been rescheduled for 3:00 a.m. the next day. I needed some rest. I hung my rain jacket on a nail to dry, opened my umbrella, and spread my soggy jeans and t-shirt on the extra bed, hoping they would be dry enough to be worn again in a few hours. I spread my belongings on the spare bed, climbed under my mosquito netting, and turned off the giant heavy portable light Jake's wife had brought over.

I fell asleep, exhausted. I had visions of seeing the volcano at sunrise. All was well until I heard scritch scratch, scritch scratch. What's that? I didn't want to get out of bed to turn on the portable light, so I turned on my tiny reading lamp for my Kindle. Nothing, except the small roach in bed with me. I lifted the mosquito netting and flicked him out of my bed.

I tried to go back to sleep. Then I heard sounds of rustling plastic on the bed next to me. I clapped and shouted, "Go away." I heard a thunk that sounded like the weight of a cat jumping off a counter it shouldn't be on. Oh no!

I tried to go back to sleep. This time, I had my reading lamp in my hand, and when I heard noises, I turned it on quickly. Maybe I would have been better off thinking the family cat had come to visit me because what I actually saw gave me a small shiver. Rat number one was running across the top wallboard near the roof, while rat number two was scurrying along mid-wall close to the extra bed. Ick. And to imagine those critters were running all over my stuff!

Now, I slept in a treehouse once before in Florida, and I specifically remember them telling me, "No food in the treehouse because food attracts critters." Guess what? Yep, I had a package of crackers sealed in my backpack. They couldn't get to them, but that's what drew them in! My alarm was set for 2:00 a.m., and it was already 1:30, so I turned on the light and decided to get up for good.

Between the pouring rain, the miscellaneous critters, and a very short night, sleeping in a treehouse didn't turn out to be the kind of thrill I originally envisioned. Hey, it's all part of the adventure, right?

Yasur's Early Morning Growl

I got dressed for my rescheduled 3:00 a.m. sunrise tour of Mount Yasur Volcano. My driver, Jake, who also owns the treehouse where I was staying, grumbled about getting up so early. I looked at it like getting up early for a fishing tournament. We arrived at Yasur Volcano at 3:00 a.m. with misty conditions but no rain. Another tourist and a guide were waiting in the lot for a ride to the parking area up the side of the volcano. "Hop in." The other tourist, Meili, and I had met at the airport the previous day. Cool!

It was a 20-minute drive up the side of the volcano to the parking area. Meili and I, with our guide, set off on foot headed for the rim of Mount Yasur. Meanwhile, Jake settled in for a three-hour nap.

Mount Yasur is famous because it is approachable on foot. It has also been erupting continuously for several hundred years. It is known as the "Lighthouse of the Pacific" and is part of the "Pacific Ring of Fire." As one of the world's most active volcanoes, it erupts several times per hour. The last big eruption was in November 2013.

It was amazing to be standing this close to so much power! I could feel tiny specks of ash, like ground black pepper, landing on my rain jacket. There was also a sulfur smell in the air. Occasionally, when the wind blew just right, I had to pull my t-shirt up over my nose and mouth because of the smell and ashes.

There are several vents where we could see the bright red-orange of the burning lava inside. The wind would blow little red embers up and away until they were extinguished. About every 20 minutes or so, there would be a small rumble growing into a loud growling as Yasur did her thing! Then, Meili and I would peer closely into the crater, watching the fireworks display. Twice, we saw the red embers shoot up into the air!

Because it was misting, there was a huge cloud of steam that formed when the water hit the hot lava. The ash particles in the air made some great red photos, but mostly we were seeing steam clouds with the occasional burst of fire.

The very best part? The growling, grumbling rumble of the earth and knowing we were 90% safe while being witnesses to this amazing part of nature!

Cannibal Performance: A Walk on the Wild Side

I still had some time after the amazing visit to Yasur Volcano before I had to go back to the airport. I also wanted to snorkel at the Blue Cave, but the weather was terrible, and sunshine was needed for the full effect of the grotto, so that was out. My driver suggested the "Warrior Performance," also known as the "Cannibal Performance." Sure, why not?

I had just changed out of my soggy jeans and T-shirt and put on fresh, dry shorts and a top (thankfully not white) for my airplane ride home. It was raining when we pulled up to an empty parking area surrounded by mangroves. I asked where the village was for viewing this performance. He said, "You'll see. Have your camera ready." "Are you coming with me?" He pointed to the entrance and said, "No, I'll take a nap. See you in one hour." Alrighty then.

I went through a dark, tangled passage in the mangroves that was so narrow I had to turn sideways and collapse my umbrella. I brushed a couple of spiderwebs off my face and pictured my story on Dateline or 20/20. This was the second time on my trip that I got the willies.

I did NOT have my camera ready because I was busy picking my way through mud and mangroves, hoping there were no spiders in those webs. When I emerged on the other side of the tunnel, eight yelling kids between the ages of five and thirteen jumped out at me. They had paint on their faces and were wearing skirts made of grass. Each was either pointing a bamboo stick at me or beating it against the trees and muddy ground to make a lot of noise. Mud was flying everywhere. So much for putting on clean clothes!

After my heart settled down and I realized it was part of the performance, a teenage girl, also wearing a grass costume, introduced herself. She said that in the olden times, if I had entered their space uninvited, I would have been eaten. Oh my.

The show continued with more mud splashing, banging, and storytelling. I was led to a hut so I could meet the chief. NO photos would be allowed of the chief because he was a holy man. Black paint was put on my face, and I was led to the chief's hut. Hey, I knew that guy. We had spent half a day together the previous day. He was a relative of my driver and had hitched a ride in the truck I was a passenger in!

When the play was finished, "the chief" and I hugged, and I showed him the photos I had taken with him the day before. All the young "cannibals" gathered around to enjoy the pics on my phone. The group sang to me before I left. Very cute. I came in scared and left happy knowing I made a 1500 vatu donation (entry fee) for their humble village.

Nice performance, everyone! Had me thinking I was going into a pot over a fire...

Everything's Closed

One day, I hopped on a "B" bus and headed to the post office. On the way, the driver asked if I needed a guide for the next few days. I told him I needed one right now! We set up the day's program and negotiated a price. Off we went!

The first stop was a store to buy a snorkel... check. My main goal for the day was the WWII Relic Museum and snorkeling at the American Corsair plane wreck.

On the way, my driver made several bonus stops. He dropped me off at the Mele Cascade Waterfall, but 10 minutes later, I was back at the van because it was closed due to flooding. Darn!

Next, he dropped me at "Survivor Beach" for tea and picking up seashells in the rain. Nice.

We pulled up in front of the "Rust in Peace" WWII Museum, and I prepared my entrance fee. Closed. The driver honked the horn several times, and local people came out to tell us the owner lived on the other side of the village and that it would take some time to go find him and for him to walk over. Pass.

Then, we visited Top Rock but had to park on the road because the parking lot was flooded. Closed. The owner said it was too dangerous for snorkeling because of the heavy rain. I paid half-price admission to walk up for the view, and that was totally worth it. I enjoyed an order of hot chips (French fries) on a rainy day under cover.

Finally, we made it to the WWII Relic Museum and wreck. Closed. Nobody was around anywhere! It looked like the cyclone from last year had wiped out the Museum. We found the little aluminum boat that takes people to the wreck site, but it too looked like it hadn't been used in a while. Darn.

My driver then took me to the Hot Springs where his sister-in-law worked. Closed, but with a single phone call, it was open. I relaxed with a mud bath and sat in the outdoor hot thermal pools. Nice.

Our last stop was the Blue Lagoon. We rushed to get there before they closed at 5:00. When we arrived at 4:15, they had already closed for the day because of the bad weather. Oh man!

Well, for a day of everything being closed, I sure did get to see a lot! We made a circle around the entire island, and I got some great photos, so the day was not a total bust!

When Good Intentions Backfire

Marcus was my all-day driver the previous day. He did a great job, we got along well, and we both ended the day happy. We talked about him driving me on other excursions. I told him that I really wanted to go fishing.

Marcus said he knew a guy. Everybody here knows everybody, so I thought it was my lucky day! We haggled a bit and finally agreed that 10,000 vatu would get me four hours of local fishing from a boat and a ride to and from the turtle sanctuary after fishing. I told Marcus it was up to him how they divided the money, but the total for all was 10,000. (That was my first mistake.) He agreed. Pickup time was 8:00 am the next day.

The next morning, Marcus showed up and introduced me to his son, Eric. I started peppering Eric with questions about where we were going, what we were using for bait, and if we were trolling or handline fishing. Eric was very quiet, while Marcus just replied, "Don't worry, you will see." Uh, oh… not again!

Flashbacks to the last time I ended up hiring a tour boat captained by a guy who didn't know how to tie on a hook. It's all part of the experience, right? Immediately after I asked if we were using squid for bait, Marcus stopped at a store and ran in. He came back with our bait. Of course, I don't speak French, so I had no clue what they were saying to each other.

We got to the boat, and Marcus told me he was staying behind and asked if it was okay if I went alone with "his son." Of course, we'll meet you back at the dock in four hours. He asked, "How much are you paying for the fishing?" I reminded him that I was paying 10,000 vatu for the day, and it was up to them how they split it. (Another mistake.)

We hopped in the boat to go fishing. Eric handed me a rod and reel (the only one on the boat). There wasn't even enough line to troll with. Eric explained that if Marcus had called him the day before, he would have had the boat ready, the line replaced, and mackerel for bait. He said Marcus only called him on the way to my hotel to pick me up! What? We worked out this deal around noon the previous day!

We tried trolling with a hand line and dropping down to fish with the chicken for bait. No good. We decided to boat over to Eric's house for proper fishing gear and go to a nearby market for mackerel for bait. I suggested that he should call his dad, Marcus, and have him get everything and meet us at the dock. "He's not my dad." Alrighty then.

After learning that the two men were not father and son, I decided to pry further. (Next mistake.) I asked how much he was being paid to take me out for four hours of fishing. He didn't know. Marcus would pay him when we were finished. I asked what the normal charge was for a half-day fishing. 20,000 vatu. I told him he was working on a budget rate today but couldn't disclose the amount. I asked if Marcus would be fair when paying him, and he replied, "We'll see."

We fished for five and a half hours, caught six fish for Eric's dinner, and met Marcus back at the dock. Here's where it gets tricky. At the van, as we're saying goodbye to Eric, Marcus lets me know it's time to pay for the fishing part of our day. (In my brain, I'm thinking Marcus gets 2,000 and Eric gets 8,000.) (Next mistake.) The three of us are standing feet apart when Marcus says to me, "Give him 4,000." I will ALWAYS stand up for the underdog.

I told Marcus I didn't really think that 4,000 was fair since Eric did all the work and it was his boat. I put Marcus on the spot. He said to pay him 1,000 more, and we left.

Marcus was NOT happy with me!

As we were driving to the turtle sanctuary, he expressed his frustration with me because I had promised to let THEM split the money, and I interfered. He was also mad because he didn't get to keep the fish we caught. I wanted so badly to remind him that he was cheating "his son" but decided that the way locals run their businesses is not really my business. Marcus spent the rest of our tour in silence with me except when forced to engage.

All in all, Eric was mad at Marcus for not giving him a heads-up about our fishing trip. I got cheated out of a quality fishing trip because Eric wasn't prepared. Marcus was mad at me for interfering during the splitting of the money. I got cheated out of a pleasant rest of the tour day by a grumpy driver. I have no idea if Marcus and Eric will be mad at each other after the foreigner leaves.

Lesson of the day: I should have minded my own business!

The Coconut Crab Feast

I like to try unusual foods when I'm traveling, within reason. I heard that flying fox was available in some restaurants in PNG and Vanuatu. One of my drivers also told me pigeon and coconut crab were pretty good.

I started asking around and checking the Internet for restaurants near me. You'll never believe this, but the restaurant immediately across the street from my hotel was known for its outstanding coconut crab. Forget flying fox and pigeon, I'm going with the coconut crab!

On my last day in Vanuatu, I had time to kill and errands to run. A memorable lunch was on that list. I was one of only a few midday customers, so I was seated at the best table with the nicest view of the water. Once I chose how I wanted my crab prepared (with garlic, lemon, and green onion) and which side (fried rice), I was led outside.

There was a wire cage with six large, beautiful gray and blue coconut crabs next to several open coconuts. I picked a small one, told the crab I was sorry, and thanked him for his donation. The chef carefully took him out of the cage and allowed me to take a few photos. The snapping pincers got very close to the man, and he dropped the crab. The claws can break your finger, they are so strong! Off they went to the kitchen.

Soon, the delicious platter of cut-up crab, which had turned red during the process, was placed in front of me. The sections, including both the legs and the body, were taken apart and pre-cracked for me. The internal organs were mixed with seasonings and served in a little bowl. I was given a crab cracker and pick if needed.

My mouth started watering immediately! I dug in and finished the entire crab and one-third of the fried rice! The seasoning was light and flavorful. It was a lot of work getting the crab out of the shell, but it was delicious. However, I chose not to indulge in the concoction in the little bowl; the sight and thought of the mixed internal organs was just too unappetizing for me.

I found that the coconut crab shell was harder than the king crab legs I was used to. The meat wasn't quite as sweet either, but it was still very tasty.

All in all, my decision to eat coconut crab instead of flying fox was a good one!

New Caledonia

New Caledonia is a French territory located south of Vanuatu and east of Australia in the southwest Pacific Ocean in Oceania. It is not a country and is still technically part of France. There are 140 islands with four major island clusters: Grande Terre, Loyalty Islands, Belep Islands, and Isle of Pines. The population is approximately 300,000, with 60% living in and around the capital of Nouméa on Grande Terre.

The official language is French, and I had a hard time finding people who spoke English. I used the words "Bonjour" and "Merci" a lot! The currency is the CFP franc, and $1.00 US equals 111 XPF. Driving is on the right. New Caledonia has a president who is elected by the Congress. The majority of New Caledonians are Catholic.

Walking is safe, and the bus around the city is clean, efficient, and affordable. You need a taxi, driver, or rental car to get around the island outside of the central part. Cruise ships visit Nouméa regularly. There were four ships in port during the week I was there. Someone jokingly called them "floating wallets," which made me laugh. Many of the specialty tours, such as Hop On, Hop Off buses, only operated on days when a cruise was in port. Crazy! There were also ferries to local islands.

There are two seasons here: the rainy season and the hot and humid season. I hit the rainy season. Oh well, that's why I have an umbrella!

The indigenous people of New Caledonia are the Kanak people. They are known for their intricate wood sculptures. Bougna is the traditional dish of the Kanak people. It is made of root vegetables and meat, then wrapped in banana leaves and cooked over a fire.

The main industries in New Caledonia are tourism and mining. They produce 25% of the world's nickel. They also have one of the three largest barrier reef systems in the world. The largest lagoon in the world surrounds the islands of New Caledonia and is recognized as a UNESCO World Heritage Site. Who knew?

There are many (mostly peaceful) demonstrations by the Kanak people against the French government. I watched one about voting rights, while the previous week there was a march against the fuel surcharge. The police were in full force to monitor the march and to make sure it stayed peaceful. Interesting.

The top spots I visited during the week were Tjibaou Cultural Center, Aquarium des Lagons, Anse Vata Beach to watch wing foiling (I'll explain later), Duck Island (Île aux Canards), and Port Moselle Market. My personal favorite was Amédée Island, which had amazing snorkeling. New Caledonia reminded me a lot of Réunion Island. My best tip to you: brush up on your French and update your Google Translate app!

Key Troubles at Midnight

The first 24 hours in any new country are both awe-inspiring and frustrating. My key situation was definitely the latter.

I booked my accommodation for Noumea, New Caledonia through Airbnb. It was an adorable apartment owned by a private family. Communication through the website was clear and immediate. Upon the advice of the owner, I pre-booked a ride from the airport to the apartment, which was an hour away. The driver delivered me to the given address at 11:15 pm. I hoped this was correct, standing in the middle of a neighborhood in the middle of the night with no taxis around for backup if it was wrong!

I had written down key bits of information about getting into the apartment, including having my phone ready on flashlight mode because it was nighttime. Following instructions, I found the plant-covered archway over a gate. So far, so good. That's where my luck ended.

Next, the instructions said to look for a lockbox to the right of the gate. What? Where? I didn't see anything. Then, I saw a lockbox on a tree branch and put in the code. Nothing. I thought maybe I was lining the numbers up wrong, so I moved them all up one row, then two rows. Nothing. Did

I mention it was dark and in the middle of a neighborhood with no help if I needed it? A few bad words fell out of my mouth as I stepped back to do some self-encouraging talk. That's when I saw a second lockbox! Aha! Guess what? The code worked.

Now I have a set of gate keys and apartment keys. Home free, right? Wrong! I tried both keys while jiggling them and holding my mouth just right, and one finally clicked the gate open. I moved my luggage inside the dark yard and proceeded to lock the gate behind me. After 10 minutes of trying unsuccessfully to push, pull, lift, and jiggle, I could not get it to relatch. Every time I twisted to see if it was locked, the gate came open. Finally, I just gave up and decided the first person to use the gate the next morning could figure it out.

Now, off to find apartment number 4. I used the second key to open my apartment door. Pretty easy. I moved my luggage inside, flicked on a few lights, and attempted to lock the door behind me using the same key. Are you kidding me? It wouldn't lock. Now, if a gate is unlocked, I'll get over it, but if my front door is not locked, I might not sleep soundly! So, I twisted, leaned on the door, lifted it just a smidgen, and then one time while I was lifting the handle for leverage, it locked.

At this point, I wondered, "Wouldn't it have been helpful to include a sentence in the directions about using the keys properly?"

Once I got over that hurdle, I settled in and slept like a baby! And now I knew how to lock my door. Oh, and about the front gate? I asked a neighbor, and he told me it's a "self-locking" gate. No need to do anything from the inside. Go figure...

A Windy Surprise: The Art of Wing Foiling

My first day in New Caledonia was spent wandering around. I found a grocery store and bought food for the week. I found the bus stops and learned which bus would take me to the city center. I stumbled upon an amazing aquarium and totally enjoyed it. But my biggest surprise and delight was watching the water sports at the beach near my apartment.

I couldn't believe it. There must have been 150-200 people on special wind devices. I recognized the old-style windsurf boards. Then there was a group of people on windsurf boards with a hydrofoil. This is called foil windsurfing, wind foiling, or hydrofoiling. It seemed so much faster than regular windsurfing from long ago. Pretty cool.

The thing that really caught my attention was a person standing on a foil board (a surfboard with a hydrofoil fin) and hanging onto a separate wing. The wing had an inflatable tube that was pumped full of air by the rider when they prepped the wing. I asked what these people were doing. It's called wing foiling or wing surfing and is a cross between kitesurfing, windsurfing, and surfing.

It looked complicated but fun, though I really didn't have a burning desire to try it. All I know is that it is extremely popular here and so much fun to watch. On a windy Saturday afternoon, it was like watching art on water! What a special treat.

Sunday Escape to Duck Island

I set out on a mission wearing my swimsuit and cover-up, carrying my map, underwater camera, and seashell bag. I was determined to find a beach via water taxi. I walked to the main bus stop and plopped down on the bench, attempting to read the bus schedule (in French). I deduced that a bus would arrive at either 10:03 or 10:05. I was wrong.

Around 10:20, I met an English-speaking gentleman who pointed out that the schedule had three parts: weekdays (the one I was looking at), Saturdays, and Sundays (the one I should have been checking). It showed my bus arriving at 10:34. I thanked him and continued to wait. Soon, an English-speaking woman joined our conversation. With ten minutes to kill before the bus arrived, I pulled out my map and told her of my plans. Since it was Sunday, many water taxis were closed, but she made a few phone calls and helped me find an available water taxi within walking distance.

I paid for a water taxi ride, chair, and umbrella, and within 15 minutes, I was sitting on the beach at Duck Island! I rented snorkel equipment, put on the complimentary water shoes, grabbed the noodle, and walked into the water. I was instructed to go straight out past the reef, then curve and snorkel on the outside edge of the reef. "That's where you can see the bigger fish. Don't worry, there are no sharks."

The water temperature was cooler than I expected, but I got used to it quickly. I was disappointed because most of the coral was dead or not brightly colored. There weren't nearly as many fish as I expected. And then... a shark zipped by! Holy cow, I swear I was told there were no sharks here!

I was snorkeling alone, far from shore, and nobody would know I was missing until I didn't return their gear and get my flip-flops back! Then, ready for this one? A sea snake slithered into a coral structure! That's cool when I'm with a guide, but it's flat-out scary when you're alone!

I headed back to shore and safety. I enjoyed the rest of the day reading, napping, and searching for seashells while snorkeling close to shore.

I think it must have been my lucky day because when I asked the water taxi driver what time the last ferry went back, he told me normally it was 5:00. Because it was Sunday, people came to the island to watch the sunset and listen to music. I could stay as late as 10:00 p.m.

So, I changed my plans and stayed for the relaxing sunset from my comfy beach chair with music in the background.

What an unexpected treat of a day! Sometimes the unplanned ones are absolutely the best!

Becoming a Snorkel Snob

Have you ever had one of those moments when someone tells you about something fabulous, but because you've seen, done, or eaten better things, it's a bit of a letdown? I must say that snorkeling in the Maldives, Philippines, and Seychelles has probably spoiled me for snorkeling anywhere else. But I had to give it a go anyway because people were telling me how amazing the sea turtle snorkeling was on Signal Island.

I took a water taxi to Signal Island, rented snorkel gear for the day, and set out to be amazed. I probably should have started with low expectations; then I would have been happy with the one turtle and few fish I did see. I was disappointed with the amount of dead coral and the lack of color in the remaining coral. There were colorful fish, but the numbers were much smaller than in areas alive with vibrant, healthy coral. I chalked it up to officially being a snorkel snob.

Reflecting on my three hours in the water, two things stood out. First, I hung out with a sea turtle and watched it eat with no fear of me. That was cool. Then, I got attacked by a triggerfish! He kept coming at me right up to my mask and camera, then darting away. It was crazy. He followed me around like I did something to tick him off! I later found out from a friend that I was probably too close to its nest, and it was trying to scare me away. Well, it worked!

All in all, I'm hoping for a more colorful and less dramatic snorkeling experience in the upcoming islands!

Political Demonstrations in Noumea

I was on a Hop On Hop Off bus touring Noumea. With cruise ships in port, 6,000 passengers were flooding the restaurants, shops, and beaches. The buses were crammed with cruisers, making the atmosphere lively yet chaotic.

The route was monotonous, a repetitive loop I had taken daily for six days. Just as I was about to hop off for good, I overheard a tour guide gathering his group to board a bus and return to the ship early. Curious, I asked him what was going on.

He explained that there was a peaceful demonstration by the local Kanak people in the downtown area. Roads were blocked off, and traffic was being diverted away from the activity. Intrigued, I decided to head downtown with a busload of chatty people. A couple of them were sharing text messages about the protests, adding to the sense of anticipation.

Our bus was stopped, and everyone was asked to walk back to their cruise ship. I joined them. As we approached the demonstration area, I could hear loud voices amplified by a megaphone. The sight of local Kanak people waving huge flags and marching down the street was striking. Many police officers, both on foot and in cars, followed the protestors closely.

I approached a young police officer and asked him why the Kanak people were protesting. He explained they were fighting for the right to be independent from the French and for voting rights. He assured me the demonstrations were peaceful so far.

After taking some photos, I decided to leave quickly and hopped back on the bus to head to my apartment. I struck up a conversation with the local Hop On Hop Off guide, asking for his opinion on the situation. He described it as complicated, noting that the native Kanak people and the new generation of Kanaks didn't even agree with each other. While they all wanted independence from the French, there was disagreement on who should be in charge. Today's issue was about the right for the new generation to vote.

He also mentioned ongoing demonstrations over fuel surcharges and violent protests against French ministers in late February. All these revelations surprised me, given how safe I had felt in Noumea. I hoped all differences would continue to be resolved peacefully.

Saving the Best for Last

New Caledonia offered some fun excursions, and I feel like I pretty much saw everything I could see during my weeklong stay here. My final excursion ended up being my favorite!

Earlier in the week, I had taken a water taxi to Signal Island and took a pounding in the small boat in big waves. It was cheaper but hard on the body and not at all relaxing. So, when it came time to book my excursion to Phare Amedee (Lighthouse Island), I had a choice of taking a water taxi at half the price or the Mary D, a luxury high-speed ferry. I remembered the beating my body took from the shorter water taxi ride a few days earlier and went with the Mary D!

The smooth 45-minute ferry ride was so peaceful that I fell asleep while reading my Kindle! It reminded me of the fast ferry from Fort Myers to Key West. What a difference from the water taxi!

Once on the island, I walked up the 274 stairs inside the lighthouse to check out the view from above. Magnificent turquoise water and white sand beaches!

Next, I explored the tiny island trails and beach. I found some beautiful seashells! I'm like a treasure hunter when it comes to shelling, but because of my limited space in my suitcase, I mostly photographed the shells and left them behind. I kept a few of the small pretty ones though.

The sun was shining, so it was time to snorkel. To my surprise, there were some big fish and turtles out in the grassy shallows not far from the beach. Neither were afraid of me while I snapped photos with my underwater camera. That was cool!

I heard the lunch bell ringing, so I came in, put on my cover-up and flip-flops, and walked to the picnic area. The traditional Kanak BBQ lunch consisted of a huge variety of local foods. They fed 75-100 of us and still had some food left over. Delicious!

I couldn't wait to get back into the water again to snorkel and see more turtles. I never get tired of seeing turtles!

The only reason I had to come back in was for the scheduled 2:00 glass-bottom boat ride. On this trip, we saw 12 more turtles and a shark! The guides were dropping fish food into the water, so we got to see many fish through the glass. Cool!

I had an hour left on the island, so I chilled and read my book from my lounge chair. I heard the music playing from the dock and looked at my watch with sadness because it was time to leave this beautiful island.

Wow, I really did save my best day in New Caledonia for the last!

Tonga

The country of Tonga is officially named the Kingdom of Tonga. It is made up of 171 islands (45 inhabited) located in Polynesia, part of Oceania, in the Southern Pacific Ocean. Tonga is surrounded by Fiji, Samoa, New Caledonia, and Vanuatu. The population is about 105,000, with 70% of those living on the main island of Tongatapu. The capital is Nuku'alofa. The official languages are Tongan and English. The currency here is the Pa'anga, and $1.00 US = 2.2 TOP.

Driving is on the left. There is a bus system here, but all the locals will tell you it is unreliable, and you might wait for hours for a bus to show up. Taxis or rental cars are necessary to get around the island. The man hired by my hotel for my airport transfer was also a guide and owner of a rental car business. He was well known on the island.

Tongans are very proud people and boast of their reputation as friendly and the fact that they've never been colonized (they did have a treaty of friendship with the United Kingdom). British explorer Captain Cook referred to Tonga as the "Friendly Islands" when he visited in 1773.

Because of the 19th-century arrival of missionaries, Tonga is now 98% Christian. There is a Sabbath Law in effect that states all businesses must close on Sundays so families can pray, eat, and relax together.

Tonga is governed by a king, queen, and prime minister. The Lapita (Polynesian) people inhabited Tonga 2,500 years ago and evolved into the Tongan people of today with their unique culture and language.

I heard everyone using the expression "malo" in many different situations. My guide described it this way: "malo e lelei" means "hi," but when you shorten it to just "malo," it means "hello, goodbye, thank you, be well." If ever in doubt, just say "malo."

Sports are important in Tonga. I attended a popular track meet (participants aged 12-16) in the Teufaiva Sport Stadium and witnessed the local people's devotion to the sport. Rugby is the national sport of Tonga. America has had a couple of dozen Tongan football players in the NFL.

Some of the famous sites to visit in Tonga include Ha'amonga'a Maui (stone trilithon built in 1200 AD), the Royal Palace (not open to the public, but great viewing from the road), Talamahu Market, Captain Cook's Landing Site, Three-Headed Coconut Tree, Tsunami Rock, and Flying Foxes (fruit bats).

My personal favorites were Anahulu Cave with the freshwater swimming pool, Hufangalupe Land Bridge and Beach, Oholei Beach Resort Buffet and Cultural Dance (including a fire dance), Fishing Pigs, the boat ride to Pangaimotu Island, and Mapua'a Vaea Blow Holes (over three miles of coastline with water shooting up 100 feet into the air).

Tonga is also one of the only places in the world where you can legally swim with humpback whales. I am VERY sorry I will miss this; I'll need to come back between July and October. The best place to do this is from Eua Island, which is about a two-and-a-half-hour ferry ride from Nuku'alofa.

Another exciting island to visit is Vava'u. You can fly or take the 20-hour cheap ferry to get there. Hmmm, you could take the ferry one way and fly back! Next time...

Broken Room Blues

I arrived in Tonga late on a Saturday night. I was grateful for the overpriced taxi that my hotel had arranged for my airport transfer. Checking into the hotel was effortless, and the reception was friendly. My room was on the second floor.

Exhausted from my travels, all I wanted to do was sleep. However, I couldn't get the lock on the door to engage, so I flipped the little safety lock and stuck a chair under the doorknob. No worries, I thought; they can fix it tomorrow.

I turned on the TV for company but was met with a "no signal" notification on all six channels. No worries: they can fix it tomorrow.

Hopping in the shower, I ignored the slight sulfur smell and rusty faucets. The water was hot if you used the reverse labels with hot on the right and cold on the left. The towels were clean, which was a relief.

Once in my PJs, I went to brush my teeth. The glass in the bathroom was covered in someone else's old toothpaste. I needed to use it, so I made a face and washed it. There was no bar of soap, so I dug into my suitcase for one from a previous hotel stay. The soap dish had soap slime in it from the previous guest, so I grumbled, said a few choice words, and cleaned it so I could use it. The mirror was covered with soap scum, so I wiped it down with my used towel.

I wondered what the heck I had gotten myself into. I shifted a chair to put my suitcase on and noticed all the plaster peeling off the walls, exposing the metal underneath. I questioned how stable my second-floor room was.

I opened the fridge to put my snacks inside in case there were small critters in my room. It was running full blast but was just above room temperature and had an odor to it. Ok. Snacks went into Ziploc bags instead.

I did a quick check for bedbugs and didn't see any evidence. The A/C seemed to be working okay, so I promptly fell asleep.

The next morning, everyone was super kind and friendly. I enjoyed a delicious complimentary breakfast and expressed my concerns about the door lock and TV. They came up, looked at them, and left. I told them I'd be out for the day, and they could fix them while I was gone.

Long story short... the door lock never got fixed, the TV was hit or miss, and the offer to move me to another room was out because the other rooms were worse than mine. So, what did I do? "Suck it up, Buttercup" came to mind. After talking to others about their accommodations, mine sounded pretty darn good. I didn't have the money to upgrade to the fancy hotel next door at three times the price, and I knew I would NEVER get a refund from my place.

Tipping in Tonga is not expected but is appreciated if someone goes above and beyond. I started leaving a small tip on the bed each day, thanking the cleaning staff for taking such good care of me. I was amazed at how I started getting little "extras" in my room because of this. First, it was a bar of soap, then a washcloth, and on the last day, a disposable toothbrush! Wow!

Complaining got me the cold shoulder, while encouragement and compliments gave me good customer service. Lesson learned.

Shipwreck Snorkeling and Superb Shelling

I met three solo travelers on a tour around Tonga's Tongatapu Island. During our day together, one of them mentioned he was taking the noon ferry to Pangaimotu Island the next day and invited us to join him. It sounded like a great idea.

The next day, we all met at the small rustic boat and made the (expensive) 15-minute trip to the nearby island. Once there, it was clear that the island had been hit hard by several disasters. In 2018, Cyclone Gita, a category 4 storm (with category 5 being the highest and most destructive), had wrecked many boats, which now serve as great snorkel spots. Then, COVID came along and closed businesses for the next two years. To add insult to injury, a tsunami wiped out the island resort in January 2022. Fortunately, the resort owners managed to salvage their transport boat, which we took to the island. By renting snorkel gear and transporting customers, the family was able to "limp" along. They are living in tents and makeshift shelters, still waiting for government aid.

I plopped my sarong/towel and beach bag into a chair, borrowed a noodle flotation device, put on my snorkel mask, and paddled out to the wreck site. It was kind of eerie looking at a rusty ship that was 90% underwater with just a little bit sticking up. On the boat ride over, the driver mentioned sea snakes around the wreck but tried to calm us down by reassuring us he had not seen them in the past week. What? Guess what I was thinking of the entire time I was snorkeling? Good news: no sea snakes!

The snorkeling was just okay; the water was a great temperature, and there were only about 20 guests on the entire island. I relaxed, read, swam, and snorkeled again.

The three guys went on a walk around the perimeter of the island and invited me to go along. With visions of bushwhacking through mangroves and stumbling over cyclone and tsunami debris, I declined their offer and continued reading my book. When they returned, they urged me to check it out, saying the cloud cover made for outstanding photos. I do love taking photos, so I put on my new rubber water shoes and took off. I am so glad I did!

This was the BEST part of the day! It was low tide, and the shelling was outstanding on the backside of the island.

There were hundreds of hermit crabs click-clacking over each other's shells, scrambling to get to their jobs for the day. I bent to take a photo of a purple crab, and he promptly put up his claws to ward me off. So cool! My 20-minute quick walk around the island turned into an hour and 20 minutes. The guys thought I had gotten lost. Well, I kinda did...I got lost in the joy of an isolated island of critters!

Today, I thought it would be all about the shipwrecks, but I got a pleasant nature surprise instead!

Dodging Pigs, Chickens, and Potholes, Oh My!

I found several things I wanted to do around the island of Tongatapu. I communicated with three different guides and drivers, trying to find a price that was fair for both of us. They each told me it would be much cheaper to rent a car.

I mentioned that I was renting a car to three other solo travelers that I'd been hanging out with, and they asked if they could join me and split the cost of the rental and fuel. We agreed that I would be the driver, and they would all navigate.

I didn't sleep well the night before the rental for two reasons. First, I hadn't driven a car in four months. Second, I hadn't driven on the left side of the road since visiting Christmas Island four and a half years ago. It turns out I didn't need to worry at all!

The first issue of not driving since I left home... like riding a bike, no problem. The next issue about driving on the left was corrected within the first 30 minutes of my repeating, "Stay on the left, left, stay on the left." The funniest part was when I was going to turn on the blinker and got the windshield wipers instead! Or, how about this one… going to enter the car and finding the steering wheel on the opposite side! It all worked out fine, though.

The trickiest part of driving in Tonga was the obstacle course of pigs, chickens, and dogs randomly running out in front of the car. And let's not forget the potholes, which were especially bad during the rainy season due to the constant downpours eroding the roads. Oh my! Then, there was the coconut. I tried to straddle the coconut because there were other obstacles to avoid. Guess what? Thump! Not enough clearance on our tiny car. We started laughing, "We can't even clear a coconut with this car?"

We were all so grateful to have the freedom of going where we wanted, staying as long as we wanted, and being able to share the cost. Our group of four had each paid 150 TOP to a guide two days earlier to do half of what we were doing now. Our current trip with rental and fuel ended up costing us each only 25 TOP ($11.36). That was for 12 hours and included pickups and drop-offs at the airport and ferry. What a bargain!

We all agreed it was an amazing day of adventure, fun, relaxation, and camaraderie!

Sporting Spirit in Tonga

I found myself running out of things to do in Tonga, so I went to the visitor center and asked about golfing, fishing, cultural dances, rugby, etc. The nice lady helped me with all my queries and let me know there was no rugby, but a major track meet was going on at the downtown sports stadium. Say no more. Taxi!

I arrived at the Teufaiva Sport Stadium in the early afternoon and paid the 10 TOP admission fee ($4.50 US). As I was walking into the stands looking for a place to sit, a local woman scooted over and patted the space next to her. Thanks! Soon we were friends, and I knew all about the event in front of me.

The track meet was a huge deal and very well-attended. The participants were students ages twelve to sixteen from all the island schools. The track uniforms were all matching, the stadium was covered and clean, and the track surface was well-maintained. They take their sports seriously in Tonga!

There were two little girls sitting in the stadium in front of me. One was shy, and the other was curious about the foreigner. They became my buddies as well.

The track meet was exactly like the track meets I remember as a kid. Lots of milling around and stretching. Shot put, discus, high jump, and long jump were all being held simultaneously in the center of the field, while the races were happening on the beautiful track. An announcer kept everyone informed about each competition.

There were many individual tents set up with local foods for sale. I didn't recognize most of these snacks. The little girls in front of me shared their snacks with me, and I still had no clue what I was eating.

The funniest part of my afternoon came when a race started, and the announcer cranked up the loud dance music! Many of the parents (mostly moms) stood up and started vigorously dancing! Many came out of the stands yelling for their teams while twerking and shaking pretty much every body part! Remember, most Tongan women are quite curvaceous. I was roaring with laughter at their enthusiasm! This didn't just happen once but for every race!

The most memorable part of my afternoon came when the medals were awarded to the winners. There was a box podium with three, one, and two on each section, one being higher than three and two. The medals were on a tray held by presenters wearing their best local dress. Each winner took their place on the podium and kneeled instead of standing. The main presenter took a medal from the tray, placed it around the bowed head of the winner, and gave a kiss on the cheek. This happened to each of the top three places. The recipients kept their heads humbly bowed the entire time. Wow, I loved that part of the track meet.

The track meet was scheduled to run for the next four days. I only stayed for a couple of hours, but that was enough to "feel" the Tongan energy and loyalty to their teams. After I left, I could hear people in shops and restaurants keeping up with the track meet on their phones since they couldn't be there in person.

What a fun and unexpected way to hang out with the locals in Tonga!

Fishing Pigs and the Secrets of a Shady Driver

I decided I wanted to see the "fishing pigs" because it just sounded funny. The island of Tongatapu in Tonga has many pigs and piglets running everywhere, including in front of cars. Some of these creative foragers have learned how to fish and where to get the best bang for their buck!

The lady at the visitor center told me I must go at low tide, and she gave me those times. She marked on my map one area that was walkable and one area that required a taxi.

I set off early the next morning to find these famous "fishing pigs." After walking the correct distance, I saw no pigs foraging on the shoreline. A taxi pulled up and asked where I was going. He said that there are no pigs in that area, but he would drive me to the well-known area shown on my map. We negotiated a price.

Along the way, we chit-chatted. I learned that he:

- Used to grow marijuana and sell it.
- Has six children.
- Has cheated on his wife.
- Would rather keep the 10% tithing money than give it to the church.
- Now follows a more spiritual path and doesn't do most of those things anymore.

Feeling uneasy, I took a photo of his taxi badge as a safety measure and pretended to send it to my mom while he watched. This way, he knew someone else was aware of his identity and our location. Oi.

We got to my destination a little late because my driver had to meet up with his pastor to drop off a few things on my dime. Okay.

I knew we had arrived when I saw the sign for the famous "Fishing Pigs." I saw the pigs on the muddy beach rooting around, grunting, digging in the sand with their snouts, and turning over rocks. They were finding and eating fish, crabs, and mussels for breakfast! That was one of the strangest things I've ever seen!

There were only four of them when we arrived because the tide had already changed. They were easily spooked, and after ten minutes, three of them headed back across the road toward their homes. Finished. The fourth one was chin-deep in mud and shellfish and couldn't care less if I was taking his photo. Crunch, snuff, grunt, crunch, crunch…

I hopped back in my taxi with my colorful driver and headed back to the drop-off spot (Catholic Church). He pulled over to talk to one of his buddies and asked me if it was okay if we gave him a ride. I had flashbacks to my taxi ride in Vanuatu when everyone got a free ride on my dime. It was okay since he asked.

Ready for this? Just when you thought the ride was over and my driver was reformed, we pulled over in front of the jail. My driver got out some money and walked over to one of the prisoners working in the field and handed him the cash. Of course, you know I asked. He told me he used to sell drugs with those guys, but they got caught and he didn't. So, he said he gave them money from time to time to let them know he didn't forget about them. I think there's a word for that kind of money...

I couldn't get out of the car fast enough when we pulled up to the church! He had given me his WhatsApp number and told me to contact him again if I needed another ride. Thanks for the ride. Nope, not gonna happen.

Craving Home Comforts While Exploring the World

A couple of my friends asked if I was tired of traveling or homesick. Did I miss anything from home? Well, to be honest, I think the pace I kept for the *Island-Hopping Adventure* was more like a sprint when I should have treated it like a marathon.

One of the blessings (and curses) of my high-energy personality is the ability to do and see more than the average person. I am curious by nature and absolutely do NOT want to miss out on anything! But we all must rest sometime. So, here's my answer.

Am I tired yet? I'm approximately four months into a five-month trip. I've visited 12 out of the 17 islands I planned to visit. I've stayed in 23 different accommodations and taken 29 flights, many with long layovers. Yes, I'm getting tired of all the flying and changing accommodations. I'm trying to work in some down days, but the way I scheduled the stays on each island, between seven to twelve days, often doesn't give me much time to see everything AND just hang by the pool.

Am I homesick yet? I am having the time of my life, and I would not give up this opportunity for anything, but yes, I do miss my friends and my daily routines and activities.

What am I missing from home the most? A washer and dryer! Call me crazy but sink washing and hanging clothes around the room to dry is getting a little old. I miss having the convenience of a car (my budget doesn't allow for regular car rentals). I miss salads and ice cubes! Because many of these islands have tap water that doesn't work well with our sensitive guts, avoiding ice cubes and vegetables washed in the tap water is a good idea.

I did not leave home hoping to find the same things I had at home. I came to explore and immerse myself in other cultures. I am really enjoying my experiences so far, but I think maybe five months is too long. I also think staying in one place for a longer period of time would have been better, so downtime could be enjoyed rather than viewed as stealing excursion time.

Hey, live and learn!

The Case of the Misplaced Accessories

My hotel in Tonga was a strange one. The people were very surface-friendly...until you had a concern. The hotel itself was a wreck with peeling plaster, doors that didn't lock properly, TVs that rarely worked, and rusty and stained bathrooms. BUT the hot water was consistent, the Wi-Fi worked, the A/C kept my room cool, and the free breakfasts were nice.

I thought I was being a real trooper by "sucking it up" and going with the flow of the country. As with all accommodations where I know people will be coming and going, I hid or locked away my possessions of interest, zipped cosmetic bags, and tried to remove opportunities for snooping.

It was on a Friday night when I opened my tiny jewelry purse to get my gold hoop earrings. I wanted to wear them to a buffet dinner and cultural dance. They weren't there. I took a few items out and double-checked. Gone. That's strange. I checked the bottom of the bag for a hole. Nope. I checked the bottom of the cosmetic bag. Nope. Grrr. I went to my dinner.

In the middle of the night, I sat bolt upright in bed and thought to myself, "That jewelry bag sure seemed emptier than usual. Where was my white watch?" I raced out of bed to check, and it was missing too! Dagnabbit! I tried to think of when I wore it last and remembered changing the time on it four days prior. That is NOT a coincidence that two items have been misplaced.

I wondered which other items I had misplaced. I checked my medications, and without counting pill for pill, those seemed intact. I never left my purse or phone in the room unattended. My passport was still hidden between clothes. Crap.

When it was time to check out of my room, I decided to leave a Florida postcard with kind words. I also left snacks and seashells as a gift. I even included a small tip like I'd been giving each day. Additionally, I wrote a note pleading for their help in finding my white watch and gold hoop earrings I'd "misplaced" in my room. If you find them, please let me know before I head to the airport in a few hours. Thanks again for all you did to make my stay so special. I also shared a note with the manager and showed her recent pictures of me wearing the two items.

The gold hoop earrings and white watch were only valued at about $10 each because I never travel with expensive jewelry. However, it was the offense of somebody going through my zipped cosmetic bag and taking things that was most upsetting, not the value of the items.

After checking out of my room, I stored my luggage at the front desk for a few hours before heading to the airport. I had my fingers crossed that my missing jewelry would mysteriously reappear in my luggage and be discovered once I got to my next destination. Nope. This was the first time anything had mysteriously been "misplaced."

Cook Islands

The Polynesian Cook Islands are situated in the South Pacific Ocean and are part of Oceania. There are 15 islands, with the capital, Avarua, located on Rarotonga. The islands are relatively small, covering an area of only 91 square miles. The local bus can circle the entire island of Rarotonga in one hour, including all the stops!

Most inhabitants are descendants of the Cook Island Māori and are referred to as Cook Islanders. They take pride in their reputation for taking care of one another. The primary languages spoken are English and Cook Island Māori. Among themselves, they spoke in Cook Island Māori but quickly switched to English when tourists joined the group.

The greeting "Kia orana" means "May you live long." It was written everywhere and spoken frequently, often so fluidly that it sounded like one word.

The Cook Islands were part of New Zealand until 1965, and they still rely on New Zealand for many things, including military protection. The population in the Cook Islands is around 15,000, but about 80,000 Cook Islanders live in

New Zealand, and 28,000 live in Australia. Most Cook Islanders are also citizens of New Zealand. During my week there, most of the tourists I met were from New Zealand, and the direct flight from Auckland to Rarotonga was just under four hours.

Driving here is on the left. Rugby is a very popular sport. There are also many "wandering dogs" that have homes they return to at night but have the freedom to roam during the day. Tourists are reminded not to feed them or take them back to their accommodations. If they want to help, they are asked to please donate to a local vet clinic.

Most Cook Islanders are Christians, and there are many different churches on the island. Fifty percent belong to the Cook Island Christian Church (CICC). I attended a Catholic mass during my visit.

The currency is the New Zealand Dollar, with some original Cook Island Dollars mixed in. Their value is the same, with $1.00 US equal to 1.7 NZD. I found it interesting to have both a triangular and a round $2 coin being used interchangeably. I was shown the rare $3 Cook Island paper bills, so of course, I wanted those. They are hard to find because when someone spends one, the person immediately sets it aside to keep. I found them at a couple of different banks. I traded for too many and later ended up using them as tips for meals, taxis, and room cleaning, making some people smile. Don't worry, Pop, I saved one for you!

The bus system here works great. The island is so small that the buses only go in one direction during their posted times. There are two main routes: one goes clockwise around the island and the other goes counterclockwise. The locals refer to these schedules as simply "clockwise" and "anti-clockwise." To catch the bus, you need to stand on the correct side of the road for the direction you want to travel and wave it down. A ride costs $5 NZD.

Tourism is the number one industry here. There are many resorts on this island. Black pearls are also a big industry, and fish and fruits are exported as well.

My favorite activities were the lagoon cruise with snorkeling, the Night Market, shopping for black pearls, using the sea scooter to snorkel with turtles, and yellowfin tuna fishing.

I really enjoyed the Cook Islands and would love to return someday!

Adults Only: Less Splashing, More Relaxing

I started pre-booking my accommodations long before my trip began in mid-December. I used Airbnb, Booking.com, Expedia, and other sites to find the best deals. When I found myself interested in the same resort on each site, I knew it must be "the one." I booked it, even though it said "Adults Only." I decided to interpret this as meaning there would be peace and quiet for us older tourists who didn't want to be splashed by screaming children while we were at the swim-up bar, reading, or napping in a lounge chair. Don't get me wrong, I really do like children, but sometimes it's nice to just quietly chill out.

As the time approached for my Cook Islands "Adults Only" accommodation, I began to question if I had chosen correctly. I envisioned a singles party scene with a "swipe left or right" pressure to it. Could I have misread the description? Did I naively miss the fine print? Did I agree to something I didn't realize?

I had no need to worry. As my driver took me from the airport to my resort, I saw many resorts boasting "Adults Only." Of course, there were plenty of family-friendly resorts as well, so nobody was being left out.

It turned out to be exactly what I had hoped for! Adults quietly relaxing and enjoying themselves without getting pool water splashed into their piña coladas!

Joining the Locals for Sunday Worship

I grew up in the Catholic Church but now consider myself more of a spiritual person rather than religious. In my travels around the world, I've explored and learned about many different religions. As a retired teacher, I am curious about most things, including the religious beliefs of the people I meet in faraway countries.

While I was in Tonga, I was told that I should attend a Sunday church service with the locals. However, by the time I learned that, my window of opportunity was gone. So, when I landed in the Cook Islands on a Saturday night and learned that the people had similar strong beliefs, I made a point to find a church to attend on Sunday morning.

The church I selected, mostly because of the distance and time mass was being held, was St. Joseph's Cathedral. It was only a 15-minute taxi ride, and mass was scheduled for 9:00 a.m. I put on my only dress, which was very tropical, and I hoped it would be appropriate for the occasion.

Because I would rather be 30 minutes early than one minute late, I was the first person there. That gave me time to take photos and walk around the church. There was a sign on the front door stating that mass was being held in the basement due to renovations. Darn, that was going to be part of the experience. Guess what? Being in the basement WAS part of the local experience.

Others started arriving and directed me down the stairs with a smile. Strangely, everyone chose seats in the back pews! Only a few people sat in the first three rows. I wanted to take pictures and be close to the action, so I joined the people at the front. There was a lady filming the entire service, so I didn't feel rude snapping the odd photo here and there.

Most of the local women were wearing very colorful floral dresses with beautiful hats—their Sunday best! My dress fit right in. Some of the men wore shorts, some wore pants. Footwear ranged from heels to flip-flops to barefoot. I suddenly had flashbacks to my childhood when I was checking out what everyone was wearing instead of paying attention to the priest. The only thing missing was my mom pinching me to make me pay attention! Sorry, Mom, had to mention it because I think we all got pinched by our moms during church at least once!

Mass began with words and songs in the Māori language. The song's words were listed on a big screen at the front so the congregation could follow along. I quickly picked up the phonetics of the songs that had repeating phrases and joined in with my singing. Granted, I had absolutely no idea what I was singing, but I must admit it sounded pretty.

Like the Catholic masses of my youth, the priest read or said something, and the group responded. Eighty-five percent of the mass was in Māori; the other fifteen percent was in English, which I appreciated. I even knew when to respond and what to respond with, but the Cook Islands responses are slightly different from the Catholic responses I grew up repeating. A collection bowl was passed around, and I added to it as well.

Almost everyone in church used a grass fan to keep cool. I did not get that memo because my floral dress was clinging to my sweaty body after an hour in the hot basement. I used a paper from my purse to create some moving air, but it just wasn't enough.

One other difference I noticed was the altar boy banging a drum when the priest lifted the communion wafer into the air. I remember a tinny cymbal sound for that same moment from my childhood church. Rather than having an organ to accompany the hymns, there was an entire band with guitars and ukuleles. Very nice.

What a nice morning to experience this church service with the locals. I'm so glad I made this a priority.

Restored Faith: Acts of Kindness in the Cook Islands

I was having a few doubts about mankind after witnessing a few "underbelly of society" moments in Tonga. However, those doubts totally vanished on my first full day in the Cook Islands, where I experienced four different acts of kindness.

The first act of kindness came from the receptionist at my resort. Emily graciously loaned me her artificial frangipani flower for my ear, so I'd be "church ready" for the mass I was on my way to attend. Upon my return, I handed it back to her, and she smiled and said, "You can keep it." How nice!

The next act came from Ken and Noeleen, a couple from New Zealand that I met in the pool. We chatted a bit, and they seemed like nice people. A bit later, they approached me in my lounge chair to see if I wanted to take a drive around the island and have fish and chips for lunch. Yes, of course! How generous of them to include me!

The third confirmation of the goodness in people came when I went to switch my laundry from the washer to the dryer in the resort laundry facility. My clothes were still running in the washer, while my two new friends were heading out to the car to meet me. A very nice staff member saw my frustration and asked if he could transfer them for me so I could go to lunch. Seriously? That was so kind. He asked for my room number, I gave him my laundry bag and dryer token, and off I went. When I got back, I found my laundry folded and on the table of my patio! Above and beyond customer service!

If that wasn't enough goodness for one day, there was one more item to top off the "niceness" scale. I had leftover pizza from the resort restaurant from the previous night. My room had a fridge but not a microwave. I took a chance and brought my pizza to the hostess to see if it was possible to heat it while I waited. She asked for my room number and sent me on my way. Five minutes later, there was a knock at my door, and my pizza was hot on a plate and came with silverware. Wow!

The people I met today were truly one of a kind! I'm back to believing in my 95/5 theory: 95% of all people in this world are kind.

Blew Out My Flip-Flop

For the past two years, I had been dealing with foot issues, including a broken toe, plantar fasciitis, and a strained ligament. It was recommended that I ditch all my girly flat flip-flops and start wearing quality sandals with good arch support. I chose Vionic.

For this five-month island-hopping trip, I knew I'd be walking miles and miles in flip-flops. So, I bought two brand-new pairs of Vionics (navy and black). They held up beautifully for all the walking I was doing, and I never once had a problem with my feet or back.

Then, I found myself in situations where flip-flops were not suitable, but I had no other option. I was wearing them in the ocean while traversing hard, rocky coral beaches and hiking through deep mud. I basically stretched the toe thongs to the breaking point. It wasn't the fault of the shoe; I was the one "overusing" them.

After attending Sunday Mass, in the words of Jimmy Buffet, "I blew out my flip-flop." It finally happened. The little strap that goes between the toes disconnected from the sole. Oh no!

I walked half-barefooted to a taxi and made it back to my hotel. I put on my second pair of Vionics and realized I'd stretched them out as well, and they were ready to blow any day! I asked the receptionist at my hotel if there was a shoe repair place in the Cook Islands. After laughing, she replied, "Sorry, no." Uh oh.

Two days later, I was the proud owner of very cheap, very flat replacement flip-flops. Those of us with foot issues know that's not a good thing!

I wrote to the Vionic company to see if they could repair my flip-flops if I mailed them to their manufacturer. I told them I had abused the shoes and would "foot" the bill, but I really wanted my Vionics back. Their response was that they do not repair but would reimburse me up to $20 per pair if I could find a cobbler on the islands. Well, that was nice! Now, to find a cobbler…

On my first day on the next island of Tahiti, I stopped at the Visitor Center and asked if there was a shoe repair shop nearby. You'll never believe it, but the answer was YES!

The cobbler did an outstanding job and completed the repair in one day! I now have both pairs of Vionics fixed and a reimbursement check from Vionic in the mail to my home in Florida. What a great company and what a great pair of shoes! My feet are happy once again.

Sun, Sand, and Hermit Crab Races

As part of an all-day snorkeling, coconut-tree-climbing, music-playing, BBQ-eating, and glass-bottom-boat adventure, the tour guides added one more treat: hermit crab races!

How the heck do you race hermit crabs? First, all the tourists gathered around a small circle drawn in the sand with a stick. Then, we all stepped back while a larger circle was scratched into the sand outside the small one.

One of the guides came by with a jar of recently collected, squirmy, agitated hermit crabs. He placed one crab into the palm of our hands. The little claws tickled as the crabs fought to escape. We were told to memorize the shell we were holding. Right.

Next, we all placed our tiny, energetic crabs inside the small circle. The goal was to be the owner of the crab that crossed the larger line first. Well, I don't know who coached these crabs, but they all took off in the same direction toward the palm trees! There were probably 40 of us participating in the Great Hermit Crab Race, so that means there were 40 crabs heading for the hills!

I named my crab Fred. I lost sight of Fred as the other crabs overtook him. I think he used up all his energy scratching to get out of my hand! Anyway, that was the fastest contest I've ever seen, and how the heck do they know whose crab won? They all pretty much looked the same. There sure was a lot of cheering for those couple of minutes though!

I'm not sure it really mattered who won because the prize was a high-five and bragging rights. I do know that next time I'm entered into a contest like this, I will put my crab on the line facing the woods!

Making Memories with Phase 10, Farkle, and Friends

I LOVE playing card and dice games and will play whenever I find someone who enjoys them too! I even packed six dice and a deck of cards in my limited suitcase space. I met an American couple back in Madagascar and played a game of Farkle with Ryan, but that's all there was time for.

Then, I met Ken and Noeleen from New Zealand! We got along well and even hung out together a bit. When I found out they liked to play cards too, I was beyond excited!

Our resort had a deck of Phase 10 cards (which we all knew how to play), and I brought out my dice and taught them how to play Farkle. You would have thought I was a six-year-old who was just told she was going to Disney! Both games were fun yet competitive. We played in the resort lobby with a fresh breeze coming through while a live band played oldies in the background. We finally packed it in when we all started yawning (don't laugh, but I think that was 9:30).

What a fun way to spend an evening. I was sad they had to fly home the next day. Thanks for the treat!

Rain, Rain, Go Away Already

I am tired of this rain! There has been so much rain for the past two months! I knew it was the rainy season when I booked this five-month adventure, but because I got so lucky for the first two months, I think I became spoiled.

I purchased an oversized umbrella in Réunion, then left it behind because it was too large. I bought a more compact umbrella in Madagascar, and it's almost rusted out. I got a raincoat in Taiwan and left it behind because of the bulk. I'm still toting around a rain poncho I bought in the Cook Islands when my umbrella and rain jacket couldn't handle the sideways deluge!

I've snorkeled in the rain, shopped, fished, eaten, and taken tours in the rain. I've juggled a suitcase, backpack, and umbrella in the rain on the way to or from the airport. I got used to putting every single item I carried with me in Ziploc bags! My flip-flops pretty much stay wet all the time!

I don't know how to react when there's a day that I can leave my umbrella and Ziploc bags at the accommodation.

Tours have been canceled and rescheduled many times due to the rain. Locals love it! It keeps their island lush and happy. Tourists hate it because we are stuck indoors or can't enjoy the pool or beach.

I have to say, rain or shine, unless a tour company canceled on me, I showed up every time with a smile on my face, a bit soggy maybe. I would rather take a wet, modified tour than sit in my apartment and miss out on seeing the island!

From Disappointment to Delight: Muri Night Market

I'm not complaining, because this IS a small island, but when you say "Night Market," I think of something totally different than what I saw in the Cook Islands.

Imagine hundreds of food stalls with steam spilling into the aisles. Imagine vendors selling local crafts and knock-off purses. Imagine thousands of people out enjoying a cool night, eating under the stars. That's not here.

I took the "clockwise" bus to the Muri Night Market and was super excited to graze my way through all the stalls. (I even skipped lunch so I'd have plenty of room.) I didn't really need to do that.

I think there were maybe about a dozen food stalls, two booths advertising turtle excursions, and zero craft booths. At first, I was disappointed. Then, I got an attitude adjustment and compared it to the Babcock Ranch Food Truck Friday back in Florida! I love their food trucks, but more importantly, I love the way their community comes out to mingle under the stars. It's less about the food and more about the mingling.

I carefully selected my meal and sat at one of the many plastic tables. I did some serious people-watching and thoroughly enjoyed it. I was just finishing up and walking to the entrance to wait for the bus (they only run once per hour) when the churro booth caught my eye. I had plenty of time, so I ordered a warm churro with a scoop of vanilla ice cream.

Two things happened at the same time. First, the bus arrived early, but unfortunately, they had to make a fresh batch of churros, so my order was late. I had to decide quickly: should I cancel my order and hop on the bus or stay to eat my churro? I stayed with the churro.

The guy at the counter said, "Wow, most people would have canceled their order and run to get on the bus." I told him I was there to hang out, enjoy my dessert, and read my Kindle. Anyway, another bus would come along in one hour.

Exactly one hour later, it started to rain. I hopped on the "clockwise" bus because the "anti-clockwise" bus had stopped running for the night. (That's the one I needed.) So, I rode around the island for an hour in the dark, rainy night. I was the only passenger and was distressed to see the driver continuously checking his phone. What? I kept asking him annoying questions just so he'd quit playing on his phone while he was driving.

I was so happy to be off that bus. The driver was happy too!

From Appetizers to Desserts: A Progressive Dinner Tale

Do you remember long ago when we had progressive dinners in our neighborhoods, where each couple hosted a part of the meal, and then everyone moved on to the next house for the next course? The entire evening could last between four and six hours, depending on how long you lingered at each home. I fondly remember participating in and hosting those!

Well, the Cook Islands offered that same opportunity for trying local foods, prepared by local families, and hosted in their homes! I signed up immediately!

The bus driver collected 17 of us. Most were from New Zealand, with a couple of Aussies, and then me. We arrived at the first house, which belonged to Auntie Tapu. She showed us around her gardens, introduced us to her friendly dogs and cat, and explained why her husband was buried in her yard. In the Cook Islands, many families bury their loved ones and place beautiful headstones in their yards. Since most land stays within families and can only be leased, not sold, there's no risk of outsiders inheriting family cemeteries. At first, I thought it was kind of strange, but when Auntie Tapu said she says hello to her deceased husband as she's mowing the lawn or drinking coffee outside, it actually seemed convenient. It was the first time I'd ever had to think about that!

We went inside to enjoy the appetizers prepared with fresh fruits and vegetables from her garden. We were asked to bow our heads while she blessed our food. She and her daughter described the various foods as we filled our plates. After the first round, we were all invited back for seconds while our driver, his friend, and Auntie Tapu played traditional local music for us. What a beautiful experience. And that was just the appetizer!

We all piled back onto the bus and drove to the second home. We were greeted by the family dog and Mike (Mom and Grandma prepared the food but were too shy to speak to us). After a blessing was said, we ate the main dishes, which included chicken, beef, and fish prepared with local ingredients. Everything was delicious. Mike told us about his family and life in the Cook Islands. We thanked Mike and his family for welcoming us into their home.

The third stop was the home of Tamao, and his wife, who was very shy and stayed in the shadows. Tamao had a very dry sense of humor and kept us entertained while we sampled 11 different desserts. We enjoyed local music and stories at this home as well.

Everyone got along so well, and we all enjoyed this amazing cultural experience! I loved getting a peek inside the homes and lives of Cook Islanders.

As we were all being delivered back to our separate hotels, I fondly remembered the progressive dinners from the past and smiled to myself. Maybe, just maybe, we should bring them back to our neighborhoods in America!

Zooming Underwater: Sea Scooters and Turtles

I've been snorkeling and doing so many water sports on this island adventure that my eyes lit up when I saw an excursion with something a bit different. It was turtle watching with a twist. Turtle Ariki Adventures offers snorkeling in the usual way with fins, but instead of stroking with your arms, you use a small motor called a sea scooter. Imagine holding a 2-liter bottle of soda flat in front of you with the cap pointing away. Now, imagine two handles on the sides of that bottle and a trigger on the right-side handle. Replace the soda with a motor and battery inside. That's a sea scooter.

We were briefed on how to use the sea scooters. We walked out into the lagoon, did a trial run with our snorkels, fins, and scooters. Then, off we went. There were six of us in our group, with one leader and three helpers. The staff members kept a close eye on us because the water was deep and the current strong. It got a bit confusing as two more groups of turtle tours mixed in with ours, but our guides kept us together.

I loved my little scooter! This was way better than using my arms, and I could turn so easily. I saw so many turtles! They weren't afraid of people because many people watch them every day. Some of them were low in the rocks, some came up for a breath, and others swam right next to us. How cool was that!

The staff was passing around a GoPro, taking pictures of the turtles and each of us. The sea scooters were especially nice when it was time to swim back to shore. The wind had picked up. It would have been exhausting to swim all the way back without my sea scooter. One of the staff members had a motorized raft to take people back if necessary.

What a fun, unique way of snorkeling! I thought it was going to be all about the turtles today, but for me, it was mostly about that nifty little sea scooter!

Navigating Waves and Catching Tuna

I was so excited to find a fishing charter that was within my budget! I'd been doing so much local "handline" fishing and catching tiny fish that I wondered if I'd ever catch a big fish again. Well, it finally happened in the Cook Islands when I found Captain Mau!

We both rearranged our schedules and planned to meet Friday morning, weather permitting. He generously offered to pick me up at my resort at 5:30 a.m. so we could get an early start before any possible storms.

Normally, charters like this would have three or four more guests, but when I asked how many were joining us, he replied, "Just you and me, kid." Wow, I couldn't believe my luck to get a private charter at a shared price!

We went through all the normal boat routines and were headed out of the lagoon into the open ocean by sunup. He said we were looking for FADs, which are Fish Aggregating Devices. Several had accidentally slipped into these waters and lost their beacons but still attracted tuna. Interesting.

We were also looking for birds. Circling birds meant small baitfish were being pushed to the surface by bigger feeding fish below. We found them.

I would steer the boat while he let out the lines near the FADs and birds. Bam. The first yellowfin tuna of the day was around four kilograms—not big, but fun. It took another hour to find fish at the next FAD. Bam, bam. We had two tunas on at the same time. Again, four kilograms each. Then, one last try near the birds, and we found one more yellowfin at five kilograms.

When Captain Mau clubbed our tuna before putting them on ice, a handful of tiny silver minnows scattered around the deck. So that's what the tuna and birds were eating!

As the skies turned dark and the wind picked up, the captain said, "Let's be smart. Have you had fun? If so, let's head in." Sounded smart to me. I must tell you that I was white-knuckling the handrail as we slammed into waves on the way back. I thought the waves were big going out, but coming back was semi-scary. He said the waves were three meters high. Oi.

We had to fight through the crashing waves that separated the turbulent ocean from the safe harbor of the lagoon. I experienced a new level of faith in the captain. The waves were so high and so hard that you could see through them as if they were thick panes of glass. I put my phone into my waterproof bag, said a little prayer, and held on for dear life.

Captain Mau approached the lagoon entrance, then circled back three times. I calmly asked what he was doing. He said he was counting. Ok. I silently watched the wheels in his brain turning, made a mental note of where the life jackets were, and then he powered straight through at a high speed. I didn't realize I was holding my breath until it swooshed out all at once! I looked over at the captain, gave him a fist bump, and said, "Well done!" His response, "Well, that was a bit dodgy!"

The next half hour was spent getting the boat up to the dock and then onto the trailer. Luckily, there were three men hanging around the dock who came straight over to lend a hand. One of the guys commented, "Either you're a magician or a fool." I vouched for my captain's skills.

What an exciting last day of being 59 years old!

Tahiti

Tahiti consists of two parts, Tahiti Nui (large) and Tahiti Iti (small), connected by the Taravao Isthmus. It belongs to France, is part of the Society Islands, and is in the middle of the Pacific Ocean. It is 4,100 miles from Los Angeles and 3,805 miles from Sydney. Tahiti is the largest island in French Polynesia, with a population of around 200,000. Papeete is the capital and has the only international airport in French Polynesia.

The people of Tahiti are known as Tahitians. The official language is French, but English and Tahitian are also spoken here. Driving is on the right side of the road. Most of the population is Christian. The entire population was converted to Protestantism in the 1820s, but now there are many Catholics and LDS members as well.

The currency is the CFP franc, the same as in New Caledonia. $1.00 USD equals 112 CFP francs. Most stores accept either USD or francs at a one-to-one-hundred ratio.

Tahiti is the main producer of Polynesian vegetables and fruits, such as taro, sweet potatoes, and bananas. Most of the island's income comes from agriculture, fishing, and tourism. Tahiti is the primary island visited by tourists. From my Airbnb apartment, I saw one to two cruise ships in port daily.

Tahiti was formed by volcanic activity and has mountains in the center, surrounded by coral reefs. A main road circles the entire island, with one very rough road cutting vertically through the middle. The 4x4 excursions take this route. It's a great tour, but be prepared for six and a half hours of bumps! There are many rivers and waterfalls in the lush rainforest. Due to the recent heavy rains, we saw more than 200 waterfalls on the day of our excursion.

Popular activities for visitors to Tahiti include a 4x4 safari, a ferry day trip to Moorea, shopping for black pearls, visiting the local market, taking a five-hour island highlights tour, going on a monoi oil tour, and visiting the black sand beaches.

Tahiti had been on my bucket list for a long time. I'm glad I went, but it seemed so touristy that it lost its small island appeal.

Turning 60 in Tahiti: A Birthday to Remember

When I landed in Tahiti in the middle of the afternoon, my main goal was to go out and find birthday cake somewhere. This was my actual 60th birthday, and I do like to celebrate birthdays! I did the basic things to figure out where

I was and how I would get back into my apartment upon my return, then I set out exploring.

I found several restaurants with dessert menus and had my eye on a slice of pineapple cake at one. I kept walking. Then, I heard ukulele music and was drawn to Vini Vini Fish N' Chill. Sold.

I was seated at a high-top table right next to the band and told them how excited I was to have found live music on my 60th birthday. They asked my name and said, "Happy birthday, Yvonne!" The temperature was just right, the food was delicious, and the ukulele music was soothing… what a perfect choice of restaurant for my 60th. I motioned for the bill. Nothing. I enjoyed some more music. I motioned for the bill again. I saw a nod between the band leader and the waitress.

Then, the band played the Tahitian version of the Happy Birthday song while both waitresses came to my table. One placed a blue flower behind my ear, while the other placed a scrumptious-looking mousse dessert in front of me. "Compliments of the staff, happy birthday!" I was smiling from ear to ear and thanked all of them for making my birthday away from home a special one.

Being 60 is alright after all!

A Perfect Day with Friends at the Intercontinental Tahiti

My Florida friend, Dione, and her husband, Robert, planned a trip to Tahiti to coincide with my visit. It was also the weekend of my 60th birthday, so we planned to spend a day together at their fabulous resort.

Wow! That place was incredible! They treated me to their five-star breakfast buffet. My eyes almost popped out of my head when I saw not one but two trays of bacon! One offered crispy bacon, while the other offered extra crispy bacon. I almost stopped right there, but all the other choices were calling my name too. I've never seen such variety! There was even a wall of donuts!

As the three of us settled into our seats, local dancers came up onto the stage and performed their cultural dances for us. Beautiful. They even asked for volunteers, and Dione got up on stage and looked like a professional hula dancer! I loved her courage.

After walking around the property and being amazed at all the amenities, we checked out two sets of snorkel gear and life jackets. We went back to their overwater bungalow where we put on our swimsuits. Robert wasn't in the mood to snorkel but was happy to be the photographer. Do you know how cool it is to step off your back porch into turquoise blue water filled with colorful fish? The current was strong, so we stayed close to their bungalow. Robert threw pieces of bread into the water so the fish would come closer. Pretty cool!

After snorkeling, "the girls" played a card game called Briscola while Robert snuck in a vacation nap. I opened my birthday card and told her how fabulous it was getting to spend the day together in Tahiti!

The three of us went into town for a late lunch and hung out lazily, chatting about random topics. Chillin' in Tahiti!

What a fabulous birthday treat! Thanks, guys!

The Unexpected Ferry Challenge

When I was booking flights and accommodations nine months ago, I researched transportation between the Society Islands because I planned to spend one week on each of four islands. Every site I checked quoted cheap ferry prices with no reservations needed until seventy-two hours before departure. I trusted my research and waited to book the ferries from Tahiti to Moorea to Huahine to Bora Bora, then back to Tahiti. Well, you knew there'd be a snafu, or this wouldn't be a chapter, right?

I landed in Tahiti on a weekend when things were closed, so I made Monday my day to purchase all of my ferry tickets for the month. I was in for a rude awakening! What I saw on the Internet nine months ago and what really happened DID NOT MATCH. At the ferry terminal, I asked to book my $15 ferry ticket to Moorea for the following week. No problem. I then asked to book from Moorea to Huahine. I was told there are no direct ferries from Moorea to Huahine, and I would have to come back to Papeete. Piece of cake. NOT. I quickly found out the ferries don't run every day. I prepaid all my accommodations months ago on the premise that I could just "hop on a ferry."

Now, let's book the next two legs, and I'll worry about the missing pieces when I get back to my apartment and have

Wi-Fi. I was able to book the ferry from Huahine to Bora Bora. Then, the clerk's computer froze. Oh no.

I needed to do a cost analysis of booking additional accommodation to match the ferry schedule versus booking a slightly more expensive flight and arriving on the correct day. Flying won, and I booked two flights to get to my upcoming destination islands on time.

My lesson learned from today's snafu directly relates to the carpenter's rule, "Measure twice, cut once." Mine will be, "Research multiple times, know the facts."

Tahiti's Spine-Jarring 4x4 Expedition

One of the most popular excursions in Tahiti was the 4x4 Safari. Several companies offer the same tour, and all of them warn you about the bumpiness of the ride. Well, they were not kidding!

The best part about this excursion was that it got you out of all those touristy areas. There were six of us buckled into two bench seats in the back of a 4x4 pickup truck. Five people spoke French, and only I spoke English...this was not one of those engaging tours where we all became friends and swapped numbers on WhatsApp.

Our driver took us through the middle of Tahiti Nui. We were jostled around, bumped up and down, bitten by mosquitoes, thrown sideways a few times, and rained on quite a bit. Except for the mosquitoes, I loved it! We were in the mountains!

Because there had been so much rain, there were hundreds of waterfalls! I know I saw at least two hundred. We made regular stops for photos and to walk in the water. It was not a good day for swimming, but we had our swimsuits just in case.

We stopped for a picnic where we all ate our lunches. While we were munching on our sandwiches and chips, our guide sliced up fresh local pineapple, bananas, and Tahitian grapefruit for us to share. Yum!

The back of the truck was open-air with a clear tarp for the top and sides. Part of the time, it was rolled up and we could have the wind blowing through our hair, but mostly it was down because of the rain.

This was an eight-hour tour, and six and a half hours of it was spine-jarring. It was an awesome experience, but at the same time, I was glad it was over. I don't think I could have handled much more jostling. Now I know why the ads warn you about all the bumps!

Minimalism vs. Materials: Lessons from the Road

I've been traveling with only a carry-on and a daypack for four and a half months, staying in modest apartments or hotel rooms. My clothing choices are limited to just a few outfits. I've rarely had access to a washing machine and only once a dryer. The dishes in the kitchen are basic, and I hand wash them after I cook. I haven't used a dishwasher since I left home. The furnishings are limited to what is necessary to survive comfortably: a bed, couch, chair, table, and maybe a TV. I buy only the groceries I'll need for a few days at a time.

So, that makes me wonder... do we really NEED all that stuff we have in our houses? Being away from home makes you think about priorities, space, and the organization of your belongings. Once you make do with so much less, could you live a minimalist lifestyle once you get back to a house full of things you often never use? Hmmm...

I do know this: I really miss having a car and a clothes dryer. I miss my outdoor gear (bike, boat, pickleball paddle, golf clubs, beach chair) and the opportunity to exercise with those items consistently. I wish I had my hiking pants, boots, and poles. There have been a few things I had to buy, such as water shoes, an umbrella, new flip-flops, and a watch.

I've been doing without many of these things for a very long time already, and it's been okay. But I think if I'm forced to make a choice between "Stuff vs. Minimalism," I will choose my stuff, maybe just not ALL of it. Which would you choose?

P.S. The next trip I take, I think I'll pack a bigger suitcase!

Tahiti Tour Trouble: Ant in My Eye

I was on a tour of the highlights of Tahiti Nui with a fabulous guide and two tourists from California. We were having a great time and had stopped at a grotto where we each posed in front of a bicycle decorated with flowers. I tipped the artist and walked over to stand in the refreshing water of the cave. Immediately, my upper eyelid started burning. I rubbed my eye, which only infuriated the offender. Next, the inside of my bottom eyelid felt like it was on fire. I rubbed and rubbed and squashed a tiny little ant into a black speck. Holy cow, that hurt!

My tour guide suggested splashing some cold grotto water on my eye. That helped a bit, but then my crazy brain wondered if I was exposing an open wound to a different threat of bacteria. We finished the tour of that location while my eye was watering and burning. As soon as we got to the car, I pressed a cold water bottle to the aching spot to relieve the pain. I also took two Advil to reduce inflammation and rinsed my eye with fresh bottled water. My vision became blurry in that eye. Oh no!

You know that feeling you get when something's wrong in your body, but you're not quite sure if it's serious or not? And you really don't want to look like a fool by rushing to an Emergency Room, and it turns out to be nothing. But you don't want to not go when you have the opportunity? Well, that's where I was.

The guide and other guests asked if I needed a pharmacy or a doctor, and I kept saying no, I'll give it some time. My eye felt like it did when I got stung by fire ants in Florida. I know I'm not allergic to them and that eventually, the pain goes away. I crossed my fingers that this situation was similar. I envisioned myself with a swollen-shut right eye for the rest of my vacation.

The result was all clear. Within two hours, it was back to normal with just a slight irritation, probably caused by me rubbing so hard. So, how the heck did an ant get into my eye? We all agreed that most likely it was on the flowers I posed with and got caught in my crazy hair. He likely fell as he was trying to escape the mass of frizzy curls and made a wrong turn. We both lost in that little adventure. Sorry, buddy.

Crafting My Own Infused Monoi Oil

One of the cool things about not pre-booking all my tours is finding unexpected treasures. I only learned about the Monoi Tour on the previous day's Island Highlights Tour. I took the bus from Papeete to Paparā, then made my way to the office for the tour. I was warmly greeted by a lovely local lady named Mahinae. She told me that I was the only guest for the morning. Lucky me!

Our tour started with a short ride in the company truck to the Tiare Tahiti Plantation. I was clueless about what tiare and monoi were, so the questions were flying, and Mahinae was a trooper! Here's what I learned in a nutshell:

Tiare and Tahitian gardenias are the same thing. Monoi oil is created by soaking tiare blossoms in pure coconut oil, so the gentle fragrance is infused into the oil. It is important for certification reasons that the blossoms are hand-picked before they have a chance to open into flowers. It is also important that the ratio of blossoms to coconut oil meets the standard. This company soaks 12 blossoms per liter of coconut oil. The 5,000-liter vats on the property require mesh bags holding 60,000 blossoms for a soaking period of 10 days.

The plantation we toured was 1.6 hectares in size (about 4 acres) and had 1,400 tiare shrubs. There were currently two workers for the fields, but they were in the process of bringing in young interns to help with this enormous job of caring for and picking the blossoms. I saw some corndog-shaped aluminum foil bundles on some of the lower branches of the more mature shrubs. This is how they produce more tiare shrubs:

1. Scratch the branch.

2. Place very wet mulch around the scratches.

3. Wrap that in clear thin plastic wrap.

4. Wrap that layer in aluminum foil.

5. Wait for roots to grow inside the wrap.

6. Cut the branch and put it in a pot of soil.

7. Once the baby plant is growing on its own, plant it in the ground.

It is a very interesting process!

We left the plantation and went to the Laboratory of Cosmetology. We toured where new products were created and saw many different products that use monoi oil as an ingredient. I'll have to check my shampoo and lotion bottles at home to see if they contain Polynesian monoi oil! Eighty-five percent of the monoi oil produced here is exported. Many upscale hotels use the hair and body products produced right here. I'm learning so much!

Now that I know all about monoi oil, I was able to create my own bottle of it to take home! I was led back into the main office where my tour had started and was given a restaurant-style menu. There were so many choices of infused oils to choose from. I took my little sushi-style check sheet and put an "x" next to two scents I wanted to combine. I picked pineapple and coconut for that Piña Colada smell. Mahinae pulled out an empty container and had me choose my own color spritzer top—I picked orange. The colorful oil bottles were as large as wine bottles. She reminded me of a bartender as she blended my chosen scents before pouring them into a small container. My creation was ready to take home!

What a unique and educational experience I had today! All for only $24 plus $6 bus fare. Can't beat that!

Moorea

Moorea is an island in French Polynesia, part of the Society Islands. Its name means "Yellow Lizard," though I never saw a single yellow lizard the entire week I was exploring. The island is known for its turquoise lagoon, sandy beaches, and jagged volcanic mountains.

Moorea is very small, with a population of around 16,000. It is only 10 miles across and has a 37-mile-long road that hugs the entire perimeter of the island. Without stopping, you can drive around the entire island in one hour! There is no Uber or Lyft on Moorea, the bus system is unreliable, and taxis are very expensive. I recommend renting a scooter or car for the specific days you need transportation. Most companies will deliver and pick up from your accommodations. I rented a scooter for 24 hours at a cost of $55 plus $4.50 for gas.

Google says the island is shaped like a trident, but I think it's more like a funky heart shape. Hey, "potayto, potahto," right? Because of its proximity, Moorea is known as Tahiti's

223

sister island. It is only a 30-minute ferry ride from Papeete and costs $15 one way. The ferry runs often, and many people take a trip to Moorea in the morning and return to Papeete in the late afternoon.

There are no snakes on Moorea!

Moorea is known as the "Pineapple Island," and because I love pineapples, I toured a pineapple plantation, sampled fresh pineapple juice in the factory, and ate homemade pineapple cake at the Belvedere Lookout. Belvedere Lookout is a scenic viewpoint offering breathtaking panoramic views of Cook's Bay and Opunohu Bay, making it a must-visit spot on the island.

I found Moorea to be more affordable and less touristy than Tahiti. I still saw one or two cruise ships in port while I was zipping around on my scooter, but it didn't have that "crowded" feeling like Tahiti did. Some of the favorite activities here include:

- Hiking
- Visiting Belvedere Lookout
- Snorkeling
- Walking on the bottom of the ocean in the helmet dive
- Swimming with rays and blacktip sharks
- Kayaking with turtles on your way to a motu (Tahitian word for a small island)
- Swimming at Ta'ahiamanu Beach

- Enjoying a cultural dinner and dance at Tiki Village
- Taking a tour of the Agricultural College and pineapple plantation
- Renting a scooter or e-bike to circle the island
- Taking a 4x4 tour of the rainforest in the center
- Touring the Rotui Juice Factory
- Enjoying a gorgeous sunset

Whale watching happens between July and November. I was disappointed to miss this as my visit was just before the season started.

The guidebooks all recommend taking four days to see Moorea. I was here for seven days and could easily have stayed a month. I will most certainly return to Moorea!

Neighbors in Paradise: A Warm Welcome

When I arrived at my VRBO in Moorea, I immediately fell in love! The exterior had been freshly painted white with turquoise accents. It had an outdoor kitchen and patio, an outdoor shower for rinsing off after a day at the beach, and a washing machine and drying rack outside. The inside was equally cute. I dumped my luggage, walked to the store for groceries, and then was off to explore.

I walked down to the private beach. There I found a hammock strung between two coconut trees, three lounge chairs, and a seating area made of logs. A set of stone steps led down to the beautiful lagoon. One of my neighbors was lounging in the hammock and came over to say hello. He peeled and shared his pamplemousse (Tahitian grapefruit) and chips with me. Two more neighbors came down to the beach to introduce themselves and welcome me to the neighborhood. We watched the gorgeous sunset together as everyone took turns throwing a stick for the dog.

Over the course of the week, my very friendly neighbors gave me homemade coconut cake, bunches of bananas, and more delicious grapefruit. Many neighbors would bring a snack and a beverage and gather at sunset to witness the beauty of each day's end in paradise.

I was also on the receiving end of daily morning guided kayaking in the lagoon, endless advice, and travel tips in the evenings. What fabulous and kind people I got to know here.

It felt so nice to be a "local" for a week in Moorea!

Finally, A Kayaking Adventure!

When I was packing for this adventure, I assumed there would be lots of kayaking. You know what happens when you assume... I had packed my kayaking gloves, so I'd be ready! I kayak once a week at home in Florida and am excited to kayak in turquoise water as opposed to the tea-colored water of the river I am used to.

After four months of no kayaking during this "Island Buffet," I gave up on it and used my kayaking gloves as padding when I shipped a box of stuff home. Guess what? There were free kayaks and a private beach at my VRBO in Moorea. Wouldn't you know it!

My neighbor Ben, a local, said he'd take me kayaking in our lagoon. We set out on a gorgeous two-hour paddle. The water was a bright turquoise and crystal clear. The depth was between one and four meters, and I could see all the way to the bottom! I saw coral, clams, brightly colored fish, and sea cucumbers.

Ben was in his sleek little va'a, which is an outrigger racing kayak here in the islands. He said he competes and sometimes wins. He also had an eye for spotting marine wildlife. We were searching for stingrays, turtles, and sharks. When he would spot something, he would put his finger to his lips and motion for me to quietly paddle up to where he was pointing. Magnificent!

In the other islands, when I booked a turtle or stingray experience, the animals were free to come and go, but they hung out with tourists because they were being fed. This was different. These were truly wild animals, and I was in their hood! When we'd spot some, they didn't linger hoping for food; they got the heck outta Dodge. I took zero photographs because they were just too fast. Memories became the photos of the day!

When we got back to shore, my arms were tired, and I had a huge blister forming on my thumb. But I didn't even care because it was a fantastic experience being in "real nature."

Walking on the Ocean Floor: A Helmet Dive Experience

For my 60th birthday the previous week in Tahiti, my family had sent me $100 electronically to do something fun.

I chose the "Helmet Dive" from AQUABLUE, which cost $99. Perfect!

One of the perks of this excursion was a pickup from my accommodation. This was key because I didn't have a rental car, and it was too far to walk. I was the only pickup passenger, so I had a chance to ask questions of the French captain. You'd be surprised at how much you can learn from picking the brain of a local driver!

When we arrived at the once lively Intercontinental Moorea, Captain Vainini explained how the resort went belly up after Covid and people now call it Jurassic Park. How sad. The two dive operators were still working from the premises.

A French family of four and I were given a briefing about the helmets and procedures. Then we boarded the small boat and went out to the dive site. One final briefing with the actual equipment, and then we were ready to hit the water.

Using the boat ladder, I went over the side until I was shoulder-deep in the water. Next, a bright yellow helmet with windows in front and on the sides was lowered by rope over my head. The helmet weighs 80 pounds and sits heavily on my shoulders. I continued walking down the steps until I was 20 feet below, standing on the sandy bottom of the ocean. The helmets are connected to tanks on the boat by yellow air hoses, and I could feel the air constantly blowing into the helmet. I was totally underwater, but my face was completely dry! I stepped aside for the next person to descend the ladder.

We were taught several ways to equalize the pressure in our ears. One way was to yawn, while another way was to roar like a lion, open our mouths wide, and move our jaws around. I don't know if they taught us the lion method specifically because we had children in our group, but that ended up being my preferred method! There was even room to put my hand up inside the helmet if I wanted to squeeze my nostrils, puff up some air into my closed mouth, and blow. Hey, whatever works!

One by one, everyone came into the water with helmets, and we knelt for our first experience. We passed around a small tube with holes in the side. It was filled with dead fish. Here came the fish and stingrays! They glided and fluttered all over us with the promise of being fed. This made for a fun encounter and some amazing GoPro photos by Laurent, the photographer.

We all walked/hopped like we were on the moon to a different location for more fish and stingray encounters. We moved about to several locations doing this. The water was amazingly clear, and the fish were so brightly colored! The rays were velvety smooth as they rubbed up against us like pets vying for our attention.

We got to one place where the photographer asked if we wanted to take a deep breath and remove our helmets for a quick photo, then put them back on. In the boat, when Captain Vainini had told us that this was an option, my brain already said NO. When the opportunity came, the dad did it, the mom and two kids all frantically shook their heads NO, then Laurent pointed to me. I wanted to say NO also, and just stay with dry hair and an easy excursion, BUT...

I did it! I nodded my head yes, and just did it! Now, it wasn't pretty, and the photo came out with me having chipmunk cheeks full of air and frightened eyes, but I did it. I ended up deleting that photo, but the memory of me being brave enough to try this will be stuck in my brain forever.

We headed back to the boat to unload our helmet gear. While Vainini and Laurent tidied up the gear in the boat, we had some free time to snorkel with the fish and rays.

Helmet diving was so different from normal snorkeling. It was unlike the sea scooter in the Cook Islands, and it wasn't the same as the underwater scooters I tried in Belize. This was probably the closest I'll ever get to scuba diving (I can't clear my ears below 25 feet).

What a memorable way to spend my birthday cash... thanks, awesome family!

Moorea by Scooter: A Day of Discovery

On my third full day in Moorea, I had a scooter delivered to the grocery store near my apartment. A friend had given me some birthday cash, so I used her money for this treat! Thank you!

I was given very brief instructions on how to use the cute white 50cc scooter. I signed paperwork stating that I was liable for up to $1000 in damages if something happened to it during my 24-hour rental period. The less-than-friendly owner zipped off to deliver the next scooter.

I stood in the grocery store parking lot with my island map and stared at this machine. This was NOT a guided tour with someone to show me where to go. (I will confess another of my flaws at this point: I get lost very easily and have ZERO sense of direction). It sounded like such an adventurous thing to do yesterday when I set it up, but now reality had sunk in.

Okay, I can do this!

I remembered which of the three keys unlocked the luggage compartment, so I stored my beach gear and locked it. Yay! I remembered which key lifted the seat to get the helmet out and put my purse and map in. Success. So far, so good.

I straddled the seat and went to put up the kickstand, but it wouldn't budge. The back tire was lifted up, and it looked like there were possibly two kickstands. My brain immediately flashed to the $1000 they would charge my credit card if I toppled their scooter before even leaving the parking lot! I got off, bent down, and looked at what was holding up the tire. Argggg, the indifferent scooter guy left off the basics like getting started.

I went inside the grocery store and asked a customer paying for his groceries if he could take a couple of minutes to help me. What a nice guy! He showed me how to put up the kickstand, start it, and accelerate. I learned more from this patient stranger in two minutes than I did from the pompous scooter owner in five minutes. He cautioned me to go slowly until I was comfortable. I sincerely thanked him, and off I went at a mind-blowing speed of 25 km/h!

I was only nervous for about the first 15 minutes. I went slowly and stayed far to the right so cars could pass me. The speed limit ranged from 30-60 km/h, and the max speed limit on a 50cc scooter is 45 km/h. I didn't hit 45 until after the first hour! Scaredy cat.

I intentionally made several unnecessary stops so I could practice parking, getting off, locking, leaving, and then getting back on. After three times, I was feeling confident!

With several destinations from the map in mind, I took off to see Moorea at my own pace!

My scooter adventure included the following activities:

- Visiting museums, a pineapple plantation, and a juice factory.
- Learning how to throw a javelin at the Agricultural School.
- Meeting a bunch of Americans from a cruise ship up on the Belvedere Lookout.
- Stopping at Tahiamanu Beach to find sand dollars half the size of my pinky nail.
- Eating half of a delicious pizza while sitting outside at a picnic table and giving the other half to a homeless guy.

- Taking cover inside a souvenir shop when the rain came pouring down.

- Buying a snorkel and hanging out at a popular snorkel beach. I enjoyed the underwater scene, then packed up while watching the sunset.

I pulled up at the gas station near my scooter rental place and filled up the tank so I could return it full the next morning. Ready for this? It cost $4.40 for riding an entire day and making the full loop around Moorea. What a bargain!

I made it back to my apartment before it was dark, locked up the scooter for the night, then returned it the next morning.

What an awesome way to see Moorea! It only takes one hour to drive the entire loop around this small island, but it took me nine hours because of all my fabulous stops!

The day that started out near tears ended with a giant, satisfied smile! Glad I gave it a go!

I Flipped My Kayak

On my third morning of kayaking in the lagoon by my house, my buddy Ben looked at me to see if I wanted to go snorkeling. Of course, I do! But we're far from shore, and I can't just walk my kayak out from the sand, sit in it, and gently paddle away. I'd have to get in and out of the kayak from the water.

Here comes confession time. I love the water, but I have a healthy respect for it too. Some might say I fear deep water, but that's not true. If you give me a life jacket or noodle, I'm often the first one in. My obstacle would be my lack of confidence to stay afloat in deep water without a flotation device. There, that explains it in a nutshell.

I tried to explain to my French-speaking friend that I didn't know how to get in and out of a kayak in the middle of the ocean. We paddled to an area that was waist-deep, where I slowly slipped out of the kayak, snorkeled, then ungracefully plopped my body back into the kayak. I think my friend either rolled his eyes or laughed, but I threw my arms into the air and cheered at my own success!

Alrighty then, if I did it once, surely, I could do it again. We stopped at another spot, which was also waist-deep, and I repeated the process! I was so proud of myself.

We were almost back home after three hours of paddling when suddenly, Ben stopped and slipped into the turquoise water for a final swim. I couldn't see the bottom, but guessed it was 10 feet deep. I hadn't been wearing a life jacket to snorkel because I had come to discover that I did float in salt water (my swimming friends have been telling me this for years!). He motioned for me to come in and swim. You remember all that confidence I had just acquired? Gone. Completely gone. I couldn't see the bottom. He reminded me I had already done it twice, and it was the same. Well, not really.

As I was slipping out of the kayak (not the part I was worried about), the darn thing flipped over! Out went my hat, sunglasses, sunscreen, and water bottle into the turquoise

234

depths. I quickly grabbed the hat and sunscreen. The water bottle was floating away, so I grabbed it too. I couldn't touch the bottom, so all my old habits outweighed my new learning. I grabbed my life jacket from the rubber straps on the back of the kayak. Once I had it strapped onto my body, I asked Ben if he could dive down to get my sunglasses while I flipped my kayak back over. Done and done. Now to get back in. Oh my. That was not pretty. As a matter of fact, when my French kayaking buddy would later retell the story to our other neighbors, he used a lot of arm-flailing gestures followed by lots of belly laughing. Thanks, Ben.

Here's my takeaway from that: I now know I CAN get back into a flipped kayak in the middle of a body of water. AND I am cheap entertainment for anyone who wants to go on an adventure with me! Win-win!

Hidden Treasures of the Tide Pools

Several evenings near sunset, I walked down to the private beach by my apartment in Moorea. I noticed that the tide was especially low. This created some tide pools in the rocks near the shore. I couldn't help but explore this newly presented shoreline.

Fish jumped and swirled near the shore as they were chased by something bigger. I even spotted the tiny, black-tipped fin of a shark that hangs out and finds its dinner near this beach.

One of the first strange creatures I spied in a tide pool was a long, snakelike creature. I asked a neighbor its name, but all he knew was that they were the "beach cleaners." I saw many of them near the shore. They had funky little fingers on one end that vacuumed the sand. I used a stick to try to pick one up, and it got thin in the middle and stretched even longer, just like a giant earthworm. Stretched out, they had to be at least three feet long. Cool.

I saw crabs with beady little red eyes and twitchy jaws. They scampered under rocks when they saw me coming. There were ghostlike fish that I could only see because they made ripples on the water. My favorite was the moray eel. It was white and covered in black polka dots. It was backed into a hole and only showed its fist-sized head. I held my camera close to the surface of the water, and it followed it with a wary look, ready to fight or flee. I took a couple of photos, then let it be. Nearby were miniature versions of the moray with heads the size of my thumb. Super cute!

I was so happy to discover these tide pools that I went down the next evening with my camera ready. I wondered what new and exciting things I'd see. Nope, the tide was just high enough to cover all the rocks and remove my miniature aquariums. Oh well, I was lucky to see what I did.

Battling Blisters: My Kayak Journey

The first day my patient and friendly neighbor Ben took me kayaking, he went easy on me with two hours of paddling. We saw so many turtles and rays that I almost forgot I hadn't paddled in four months or that I wasn't wearing gloves. The next morning, my body reminded me that I hadn't used those muscles in a while. When Ben asked if I wanted to go again, the answer was YES.

The second day was three hours of paddling, resulting in jelly arms and blisters on both thumbs. WOW! Hard to pass up those views and all those turtles zipping underneath us and rays flying through the water! I wrapped my poor blistered thumbs in Neosporin and Band-Aids overnight.

On the third day of kayaking, I was prepared for a four-hour tour! (I think my new French, hippie neighbor buddy was testing my endurance by increasing our distance every day). In anticipation of this, I had purchased some white medical bandage tape from the little store by my house.

Both thumbs were wrapped first with Band-Aids, then with the white tape. And it held!

After five days of hard paddling, my poor thumbs were ready for a break. Who knew I would finally need those silly kayaking gloves four and a half months into my trip?

Face-to-Fin: Swimming with Sharks

On one of my kayaking days with my buddy Ben, we saw many turtles, rays, and one shark. He asked if I wanted to go where the tour groups take people to swim with sharks. Duh. I followed in my kayak as he smoothly glided through the water on his sleek racing va'a. I had already been paddling for three miles in my sit-atop kayak and thought we were finished for the day. It did flash through my mind that however far we paddled out, we would also have that same distance to paddle back. Oh well, it couldn't be much farther, right? Wrong.

Ben paddled at least another mile with no breaks. I didn't want to look like an old wimpy lady, so I tried to keep up. Soon, I saw lots of activity. There were jet skis, tour boats, and even the boat taking customers out for their helmet dive like I had done a few days prior. I knew how long it took to get there because I'd been there via 4x4 and boat. Oh well, it's all to see the sharks, right?

We both hopped out of our kayaks, and I didn't flip this time! I didn't even have my snorkel mask on yet when a five-foot blacktip shark swam next to me! Really? Ben held onto our boats to keep them from floating away and urged me to hurry and get in there with them. No need to tell me twice!

Wow, wow, and wow! These were well-fed sharks and rays swimming among all the tourists. They were so relaxed, just gliding through the water without a care in the world. This was the jackpot for me! The only thing I had to watch out for were the motors of the boats as they left to take their guests to the next snorkel spot.

While kayaking, I had often seen turtles, rays, and sharks, and they were always beautiful. However, they would zip away very quickly whenever we approached.

Here it was different because I knew they were "safe," as much as wild animals can be safe, because they interacted with people daily. I felt safe lingering face-to-face and watching them in their watery world. Pretty darn cool.

When I got back to where Ben was holding the kayaks, he saw my smile stretching between my ears. He asked in his French accent, "You like?"

YES, very much, thank you, thank you!

"Now we go back," he said as he paddled pretty much nonstop for four miles. Party's over.

A Fond Farewell to Moorea

I loved Moorea! I loved where I stayed, I loved my neighbors, I loved how small and quaint the island was, and I loved the turquoise blue water and marine life. I kayaked with my neighbor, Ben, for five days. I enjoyed seven gorgeous and unique sunsets and visited the highlights of Moorea via scooter. I walked on the ocean floor with a helmet on my head. I swam with blacktip sharks and stingrays dancing through the water. I saw so many giant green turtles that I lost count. I did not want to leave!

Well, I had no choice. I had a ferry ticket, a plane ticket, a taxi scheduled to pick me up, and a management company on their way over for my checkout. I also had a bungalow on the next island waiting to prove to me that it would be just as fabulous as this one was!

I took out the trash, swept, and stripped the sheets off the bed—all the things necessary to respectfully depart my bungalow. I brought all my leftover food, such as eggs, milk, and jam, to my buddy Ben, who had taken me on the daily guided kayaking excursions. I also gifted him a six-pack of his favorite local beer with a sincere thank-you postcard from Florida. He gave me two black pearls he had found while diving. I'll never forget that old French hippie with a heart of gold!

Goodbye, Moorea! You're a keeper!

Huahine

Huahine (previously named Matairea) is an island in French Polynesia and is part of the Society Islands. It is located 108 miles northwest of Tahiti in the Pacific Ocean and is a territory of France. The locals pronounce its name "Hoo-a-he-nay," while the French say "Wa-e-nee."

Huahine is known as the "Island of Women" because it was formerly controlled by queens. The mountain ridge is even shaped like a pregnant woman!

Similar to Tahiti, Huahine has two parts. Huahine Nui is the larger part in the north, and Huahine Iti is the smaller part in the south. They are connected by a small bridge. There are eight villages. Fare is the main village in the north and is the capital of Huahine. I stayed in Maroe, pronounced "Mah-ro-eh." Be careful how you pronounce that because it has a very different meaning in French if you say it incorrectly. I know because an entire French tour group chuckled at my expense! This is a small island with a population of only 6,700 people who all seem to know each other.

You can drive around the entire island in three and a half hours. It's a giant tropical jungle. You can get to Huahine by plane (Air Tahiti) from Tahiti in a 40-minute flight, or you can take the ferry from Tahiti and arrive in three and a half hours. Speaking from experience, the ferry from Tahiti to Huahine does NOT run every day, so schedule accordingly.

The languages spoken here are Tahitian, French, and English. You will interchangeably hear "Ia Orana" (yo-rah-nah) and "Bonjour." You will also hear both "Merci" and "Mauru-ru." It all works. The residents here have a reputation for being friendly and inviting. That was certainly true of my Airbnb hosts!

Missionaries came to Huahine in the early 1800s and destroyed all the idols of ancient gods. Most of the population now follows Christianity.

Getting around the island is not easy as there isn't a public bus system. Taxis are very expensive, so renting a car or scooter is a good idea.

The main sources of income here are vanilla cultivation, fishing, tourism, melons, and copra production (drying coconuts to extract their oil).

Things to do and see in Huahine include taking the Pearl Farm tour, snorkeling, kayaking, fishing, visiting ancient temples, taking a lagoon tour, or my personal favorite, a Microlight flight. You might even get to see the giant va'a competition if you're lucky! The guidebooks recommend three days to see Huahine. I was here for one week and became bored. It's a very slow-paced island, perfect for relaxing.

A Seaside Bike Adventure

I really liked my little Airbnb bungalow in the Maore district of Huahine Iti. My hosts were super nice and right next door if I needed anything. They provided snorkel gear for my use, a bright yellow kayak, and two bikes ready for a ride (though the ocean air had given them a bit of character).

I decided to exercise my legs, so I put a bottle of water, my Kindle, and my phone in the basket attached to the handlebars of one of the bikes. I used the remote to open the front gate, and I creaked my way onto the small, but nicely paved, two-lane road.

The foam of the handlebars had disintegrated in the salty air, but I gripped them the best I could. The bike was a bit small for me, so my knees were bent more than I liked. I started pedaling with no goal in mind other than leaving my bungalow for a bit of fresh air. In previous Airbnb conversations, my host had let me know that I would need to be "sporty" to go more than 10 minutes from home on this bike. Well, I always like a good challenge, but I understood what he meant as I had to get off the bike to walk up my first gently sloping hill. I gave up on the challenge and settled for exploring two nearby tiny beaches within that 10-minute range.

I parked my bike and hung out in the shade of palm trees, reading my Kindle while listening to the gentle waves splashing onto the sand. I also saw that there were many crab holes in the grass and on the sand. I couldn't really get a good look at them because every time I got remotely close, they scampered back into their holes. It was then, as I was sitting perfectly still on a bench and not moving a muscle, that the activity began. All the crabs came out one by one to clean their homes! They were hauling little balls of mud out of their homes up to the surface! If I stayed very still, they wouldn't be bothered or threatened by me. Such cool activity once I became so still.

After being gone for three hours, my stomach began to remind me it was lunchtime. So off I pedaled back to my little bungalow. What fun watching those cute little crabs do their chores!

Nothing Fancy, Just Island Life in Huahine

Part of the upside to visiting an island like Huahine is its "remoteness." Part of the downside is also its "remoteness."

There is no public bus system, Uber and Lyft are nonexistent, taxis are incredibly expensive, and I didn't want the expense of a rental car. I had scheduled a microlight flight for one day during my stay and was chatting about transportation options with my host, Guillaume. He said, "You can ride into town with me when I go to work if you want. I leave home at 6:30 am and return at 3:00 pm." Hey, thanks!

Between our conversation and the 6:30 departure, my microlight flight was canceled. Darn. I decided to go into town and just poke around anyway. I met my host at his car in the morning and hitched a ride into town. He parked at his office building, then asked if I wanted to join him and his friends for pre-work coffee at the local cafe. YES! We had sandwiches, coffee, juice, and great conversation.

As we parted to start our day, he told me they meet for lunch at 11:30 at the same cafe every day, and I was invited to join them. Cool.

I bid a good day to Guillaume and set off to explore the capital city of Fare. That didn't take long. I think it took one hour to pop in and out of every store and walk every aisle of the grocery store. I'd better slow it down because there were a lot of hours between 7:30 and 2:30!

I found a breezy cafe on the waterfront and read my Kindle for an hour. I walked through the shops again at a snail's pace. I paid one dollar for four tiny finger bananas at a roadside fruit stand. I did some people-watching and used my time to get some exercise. I hung out and watched three dogs playing in the surf chasing fish, and I was lucky enough to watch a school va'a competition.

I walked back to the same cafe for lunch at 11:30 and ate a burger with my host, Guillaume, and his wife, Purotu. Such amazing people. After lunch, the wife headed home, the husband back to work, and I headed to the beach with my snorkel gear. Guillaume told me to be at his office at 2:30 if I wanted a ride back to my Airbnb (next door to his house). See you then!

This was a day spent "local style." I didn't do anything fancy, see any important historical sites, or do anything worthy of an Instagram post. I just did Huahine things. Not a bad day at all...

Educational Tour of Huahine's Pearl Farm

I love educational tours, so when I saw the Pearl Farm Tour offered in Huahine, I knew it would be a visit I had to take. I had taken a pearl farm tour in Broome, Australia 16 years ago, but I've since forgotten much, so this was exciting for me!

I was in luck, as this tour was included in my lagoon tour, so I didn't have to worry about transportation. We had only about half an hour to learn about how pearls are cultivated and to browse the shop. I spent 29 minutes learning and only one minute shopping (though I couldn't afford anything in the store anyway).

The Pearl Farm office and store were in the middle of the lagoon and were only accessible by boat. The farm has a small boat that transports people free of charge every 15 minutes to and from shore. Since I was already on a lagoon tour boat, we tied off at the dock.

The demonstration was offered in French and English, thankfully. (I really should have learned some basic French before this trip!) Since I was the only person needing the English version, I was able to ask all the silly questions I wanted without fear of monopolizing our guide's time!

Building the perfect pearl takes a lot of work, time, and luck. That's why they are so expensive! Pearls are essentially formed when an oyster tries to expel a foreign object like sand, grit, or a purposely placed spherical bead inside its shell. It all starts with an oyster; the inside lining of the oyster shell determines the color of the pearl. To begin the process, a nucleus (a spherical shell bead) and a piece of "mantle" from another oyster are needed. The mantle is the dark outer ring on the inside of the oyster. Tiny pieces are cut from a donor oyster and used in "seeding" pearl-producing oysters. During the demonstration, the lady used tweezers to pick up this slimy one-centimeter square chunk of mollusk.

The nucleus comes in four different sizes (2mm, 3mm, 4mm, and 5mm). I asked the guide if those were plastic beads. "No!" These polished spheres are made from shells of freshwater Mississippi mussels. I never knew that!!!

The recipient oyster is delicately pried apart with just enough room to slide in the graft and nucleus. If it's opened too far, it can harm the healthy oyster.

And where exactly do you put these two items inside the oyster? Ready for this? In the gonad (reproductive organ)! Ouch!

The oyster is then closed again and slipped inside a small mesh bag before being returned to the water. Apparently, oysters don't want irritants in their gonads (go figure) and try everything possible to expel them! If they succeed, the nucleus is caught in the bag and no pearl forms. If it stays put, the oyster secretes thousands of layers of nacre (also known as mother of pearl) over the nucleus.

The pearl farm here harvests every 18 months. If a young oyster produces a nice pearl in the first 18-month cycle, it is then given a larger nucleus to try again for a larger pearl in another 18 months. This process continues up to the maximum size nucleus.

Pearls are sold based on size, shape, luster, surface quality, and nacre quality. When two or more pearls are used in a piece of jewelry, another important factor is how well they match.

Now I understand why cultured pearls are so expensive, and why they call it pearl farming!

Thumbs Up: The Art of Hitchhiking in Huahine

My Airbnb is far from restaurants, grocery stores, and activities. The bicycle at my Airbnb has seen better days and is only suitable for short rides, certainly not the long trip to the airport. I needed a ride to the airport and back for my microlight flight. I didn't want to spend $80.00 on a taxi, so I got creative! My Airbnb hosts and several other locals said it's very safe to "thumb it" here. Yes, I decided to go hitchhiking!

I left my Airbnb allowing three hours and 40 minutes to get to my destination, which was 40 minutes away. I packed an umbrella and my patience. I informed my hosts of my intentions... you know, just in case.

I started walking. Hey, this is good exercise. I'll just walk until I have the courage to stick my thumb out. Then, the clouds moved in, and it started to sprinkle. Well, that was the push I needed, so I stuck out my thumb, and the very first car stopped.

Wow, if I had known it was going to be this easy, I wouldn't have lost sleep over this experiment last night, and I wouldn't have walked those one and a half miles in my flip-flops just then.

The driver was a high school sports teacher on her way into town for work. She was part of a four-year teaching program, and she and her family would return to France the following year. We had a nice chat, and she dropped me off in the town of Fare. Thanks. I couldn't have asked for a better first ride!

I had some time to kill since things were going so smoothly. I walked around town, had a nice lunch outside, and watched a man in a small boat come in with a giant marlin he had caught.

I left town and started walking toward the airport. There was a well-maintained sidewalk next to the road, so I was never in danger of being hit by a car. I had walked about a mile when I realized it wasn't clear to me exactly how far from town the airport was. Different people told me anywhere from eight minutes to thirty minutes. When I hit the two-mile mark and the sky turned dark again, I stuck out my thumb.

My brain said I'd crawl into the first car that came by, we'd have a lovely chat, and they'd drop me at the airport. Do you know how crushing it is to your self-esteem when people go around you without stopping? Do I look like a criminal? This didn't happen just once, but several times. Oh my. I kept walking. That $40.00 taxi was sounding better all the time. Finally, when I was almost at the airport, I caught a ride.

I finished my AMAZING microlight flight 45 minutes later than expected. Now, to hitchhike home before it gets dark!

My first ride was with a local couple (very nice) who dropped me off in town. They knew my Airbnb hosts. The next ride was from two French guys (tourists with limited English). They asked if it was okay to stop on the way to snap a couple of sunset pics. Sure, I'll take some too. They waved goodbye, and I took off walking again.

The next ride was a local man on his way home from work. I told him I was heading to Guillaume and Purotu's place. He knew them also. As a matter of fact, he intended to drop me at the bridge between Huahine Nui and Iti, but since Guillaume was his friend, he said he'd drive me the final three kilometers. No need, because as we approached the bridge, he asked, "Hey, isn't that the boss' wife there in the blue car?"

Sure enough, Guillaume's wife Purotu was worried when I wasn't home by 5:30, so she set out to look for me! What a sweetheart! I thanked ride number five and hopped in with my kindhearted host.

The hitchhiking experiment proved to me that the kindness of strangers on Huahine is abundant, and I met some interesting people. It also showed me how unpredictable and time-consuming hitchhiking is. A taxi would have cost $40.00 each way and lasted 40 minutes. Instead, I burned up triple the time, walked a total of six miles, and climbed in and out of six strange cars. I lost a bit of sleep the previous night wondering if I would meet that one random person that would land me on an episode of Dateline or 20/20. Plus, there was the bit of self-doubt, "Why didn't they pick me up?"

My takeaway from this? Been there, done that, hire a taxi next time.

Huahine from Above: My Microlight Flight

I couldn't find many excursions offered on the island of Huahine. When I discovered a microlight flight from Tahiti Air Lagon, I immediately booked it. It was a 35-minute flight in a tiny airplane, looking down over the island. It sounded perfect to me!

The flight was rescheduled once and had a slight delay on the actual day, but that happens when an activity is at the mercy of Mother Nature. After a lot of walking and hitchhiking to get to the airport, I made it with time to spare. My pilot, Antoine, met me at the airport cafeteria wearing his yellow safety vest and red ball cap, just as he described in his confirmation email. I smiled a giant smile because I knew the experience would NOT be canceled at that point. Yippee!

I donned a matching yellow safety vest, and we walked out to the adorable turquoise and white mini-plane. The painting on the side of the plane resembled the tattoos of Tahitian men. We took the customary tourist photos and then put on life jackets. What? Seriously, we're wearing life jackets to go flying? OK.

Antoine showed me (with limited English) how to "fold" myself into the passenger seat—butt first, duck your head, then one leg at a time, then unfold. Seatbelts on, radio the tower, and we were off!

Wow!!! It had rained all morning, and the wind was still strong, so I was expecting some serious bumping around. This ride was extremely smooth, and Antoine' 20 years of flying experience really showed. My lack of French and his lack of English didn't matter because the views spoke for themselves! Wow!

I saw where the Pacific Ocean waves crashed onto the white sandy beach or the lagoon surrounding the island. I saw motus (baby islands), a va'a competition, the now-vacant Intercontinental overwater bungalows, and my Airbnb. The different shades of blue were incredible. This reminded me of the small plane ride down to Key West, but even more colorful! I can't come close to describing how magnificent the views were from up above. The flight wound up lasting 50 minutes instead of 35, maybe because he had run late and made me wait, or maybe because he saw how appreciative I was of this experience.

I LOVED this experience so much! Put this one on your bucket list!

Bora Bora

Bora Bora is one of 118 islands in French Polynesia, a part of France, located northwest of Tahiti. It belongs to a group of nine Society Islands. The island comprises three villages: Anau, Faanui, and the capital, Vaitape. Originally named Vavau, then Pora Pora, and finally Bora Bora, its current name resulted from a mispronunciation since there is no "B" in the 13-letter Tahitian alphabet. Someone once mispronounced it, and it stuck. Go figure!

The island has approximately 12,000 residents, with half of them under the age of 20. French, Tahitian, and English are commonly spoken. Two frequently used phrases are "Ia orana" (hello) and "Maururu" (thank you).

Bora Bora has no public transportation system. However, it is safe to walk, bicycle, ride a scooter, rent a car, or take a taxi. The road around the island's perimeter is flat and 32 kilometers (19 miles) long. Biking around the entire island is feasible, with only one small hill requiring a dismount. The highest point on the island is Mt. Otemanu, a dormant volcano at 727 meters.

Bora Bora is renowned for its overwater bungalows, which originated here, and is a popular luxury vacation spot. The island is surrounded by a vibrant turquoise lagoon protected by a coral reef. Bora Bora is essentially a main island with a central lagoon encircled by smaller islands called motus. These motus are the remnants of the outer rim of an ancient volcano, creating a stunning contrast between the lush green volcanic island and the surrounding clear blue waters. Why is the water so blue? There are three reasons: the lagoon is very shallow, there is no plankton, and the sand is heavy so there is less churning; therefore, it stays clear.

Despite its popularity, Bora Bora receives fewer visitors annually than Hawaii does in ten days. The airport is located on one of the motus. Built by the Americans during WWII, the airport is accessible via a 15-minute ferry ride included in the airline ticket price. It's not an international airport, so you need to first fly into Papeete.

Fun Facts:

- There are no poisonous snakes or insects.
- Non-native animals include cows, dogs, goats, chickens, and pigs.
- Relatives are buried in backyards as there are no public cemeteries.
- The Tahitian gardenia is the national flower.
- Tattooing is a sacred art, seen as a sign of beauty.
- Bora Bora produces black pearls from black-lipped oysters.

- The movie "Couples Retreat" was filmed here.
- There is no hospital; for medical emergencies, you must travel to Raiatea.
- The wet season is November-April, while the dry season is May-October.
- Captain James Cook stumbled upon Bora Bora, and later missionaries converted the Polynesians to Christianity.

Bora Bora was once a military supply base for WWII. There are still cannons and 100 bunkers left by the Americans. The airstrip is still in use as the current airport. There are also descendants from the G.I.s. Between 60-70 children fathered by American soldiers were left behind after the war. I met one of the granddaughters of a soldier. Most are proud of this heritage.

The national dish is Poisson Cru, made of raw tuna or Mahi Mahi, lime juice, vegetables, and fresh coconut milk. Like ceviche, it is a popular dish throughout French Polynesia.

Favorite activities in Bora Bora include helmet diving, scuba diving, jet skiing, lagoon tours, snorkeling with sharks and stingrays, quad tours, biking, and swimming at Matira Beach. You can also enjoy 4x4 tours to see Mt. Otemanu and WWII remnants, as well as sailing, fishing, kayaking, and renting electric fun cars.

I really liked Bora Bora and will certainly return!

The Four-Minute Shower Challenge

Anytime I enter a new accommodation, it takes a bit to settle in, figure out where things go, what I'll need to buy, and find the quirks. EVERY place has at least one quirk. This one was the four-minute shower.

You ask, "How do you know it's four minutes?" I learned the hard way. First, I turned on the water to let it warm up (one minute). Then, I rinsed out the laundry I'd washed in the sink (two minutes). Next, I was in the middle of soaking my body and shampooing my hair (one minute) when I had to keep moving the temperature handle over, over, over. Freezing cold water! Brrr!

At this point, I jumped out from under the spray and had to make some decisions. Do I really need to put conditioner in my hair? Yes. Will my skin dry out if I don't totally remove all the soap suds? Yes. Forget shaving... that was an easy one.

Alright, I gently splashed the water one handful at a time on all the important bits. I stuck my head under the stream, let out an expletive, worked in the conditioner, stuck my head back under, and finished the job.

I was suddenly transported back to Taiwan where my Airbnb had a limited capacity water heater of five minutes per shower.

Plan B for the next shower: save the laundry rinsing for last because that can easily be done with cold water. Shower like you wash a car—wet everything down, turn off the spray nozzle while you scrub with soap, then rinse. Shaving might be optional this week!

All good. I know I'll appreciate my shower at home more than ever!

Inventive Fun: Plastic Bag Kites

On Sundays in Bora Bora, everything is closed. Everyone spends the day at church, eating, playing with family, and just chilling. I decided to go for a bike ride to scope out things to do later.

On my way into town, I thought I saw some kids flying kites. The kites were so small that I figured I must have misinterpreted what I was seeing.

On my way back to my Airbnb a couple of hours later, I saw another kid flying something small. I couldn't stand not knowing, so I pedaled my bike across the field and asked what they were flying. There were probably six kids (ages eight to ten) sitting in the shade, one kid around ten with the small green kite, and an older kid around fifteen supervising. The older kid spoke English and was very friendly.

I asked if that was a kite. He said, "No, it's a plastic bag." Sure enough, it was a thin green plastic bag from a store. It had been cut open, half of it taped to two sticks in the form of a cross, and the top edges folded over and taped. It was basically in the shape of a stick house drawn by a first grader. The other half of the bag was cut into long thin strips and tied together to make a tail.

Ready for the creative part? The kid was using a fishing rod and reel to let the line out!

I snapped a few quick photos and then asked if I could video the process. They were delighted to show off their free fun! That little plastic bag could really fly. How cool was that?

My brain flashed back to all the games we played when I was a kid. We made stuff up, built our own fun, and were very creative. We were outdoors. Today's little unexpected treat made my heart happy.

Biking the Beautiful Bora Bora

What was I thinking? When I woke up that morning, I planned to ride my cruiser bicycle to the beach, which was a seven-kilometer round trip. Later in the day, I planned to ride my bike in the other direction into town for some errands, which was a five-kilometer round trip. That would make my total for the day 12 kilometers. I saw my host on the way out, and he suggested that I might as well just ride around the entire island because it was only 32 kilometers in total. Wow, it sounded like such a great idea! What could possibly go wrong?

I had already put on my swimsuit and cover-up and packed my bag with a snorkel and a bottle of water, so I just threw in one more bottle. My host showed me some important landmarks on his iPad, plus I had my map of the island. He recommended that I travel clockwise, so the beach would be my last big stop to cool off. I was off!

I made it into town with no problem. After riding another five kilometers, I realized that it was a terrible idea to ride a bike 19 miles with the elastic of a swimsuit digging into my butt cheeks. Ouch.

After ten kilometers, my hands were killing me. The handlebars on the bike had a foamy black covering that was pushed far down, so the metal inside was the part my hands held onto. Without gloves, that was hot, sweaty, and painful with the rough metal end uncovered. I stopped at a hardware store to see if I could purchase something to cover the ends. One of the workers tugged, pulled, and twisted the foam and stretched it back to cover the exposed metal. Thank you! That lasted two kilometers, but without something to make it stay in place, it went right back to where it was. Oh well, we tried.

I stopped by the beaches, took a break to smell the flowers, purchased a coconut ball—a sweet, chewy dessert made from grated coconut and sugar—from a roadside stand, took many pictures, and rested my legs. One of my favorite breaks was a hike up to see the United States bunker and cannons from World War II. I eventually made it all around the island to the beach, where I rented a lounge chair for three hours before pedaling back to my Airbnb.

I finished the 19-mile loop on my lime green cruiser. I'm happy. I did it! But I have no desire to do it again.

Bora Bora Sights from an Electric Fun Car

After riding a bike around the entire island the previous day, I was really looking forward to some sightseeing that didn't involve strenuous exercise! I rented an "Electric Fun Car" from Avis from 8:30 AM to 4:30 PM, with a range of 92 kilometers. The island of Bora Bora is 32 kilometers around its perimeter, so I was good to go.

Avis was supposed to deliver my fun car to my Airbnb bungalow, but when they didn't show up, my fabulous host offered to drive me into town to their rental office. Thanks, Stanley! It turns out Avis had mistakenly entered my reservation for the day prior. This is where my organizational skills came in handy because I showed them a screenshot of my voucher. They quickly scrambled, and twenty minutes later (I'm sure someone from the back made a frantic run to their other rental office), my car was ready for me.

It took three minutes to show me how to drive the tiny car, which looked like a grown-up version of the Little Tikes car we had as kids. There was one seat in front and one seat behind with zero legroom. I think the passenger's legs were meant to go beside the driver, like bobsledding. The door opened up instead of out, similar to a Lamborghini.

The battery gauge of the car had ten bars with no mileage indicator. After burning three bars in the first hour, I knew I'd have to be conservative. I had rented the car for eight hours and didn't want to run out of juice in two!

The car was smaller than a golf cart, rough like a four-wheeler, and made a high-pitched wheezing sound like a hair dryer. That was annoying. On one stretch, when nobody was behind me, I let off the accelerator, accelerated, let off, and so on, which made a weird sort of music. Throw in the blinker, which changed the annoying wheezing to a cricket chirping sound, and you'd think a playful toddler was driving. Okay, back to serious driving.

I found out that there were three tiny fun cars like mine (no windows/no A/C) and seven side-by-side tiny fun cars (with windows and A/C) on the entire island, divided between the two Avis rental shops. I met two Americans driving one of these as we were all following the maps that came with our rental cars. For the life of us, we could not find the landmarks listed on the maps. The low battery life didn't allow for a lot of time mucking around trying to find things either. We kept running into each other at the souvenir shops, which were easy to find. Go figure.

I used my time circling the island by stopping to see things I didn't get to see by bike the previous day. The car was open to the elements. I asked what would happen if it rained, and the Avis lady basically told me I'd get wet. It also meant it was open to theft. I left unimportant things in the back seat and carried everything else with me. I stopped at stores, supermarkets, the post office, restaurants, beaches, and whatever else tickled my fancy. The car was easy to park and turned on a dime!

The little car maxed out at 47 km/h and reminded me of driving the 50cc scooter in Moorea. I got used to people passing me.

After six hours, I'd had all the "fun" I could stand. The glass sunroof, black interior, no windows, and no A/C turned me into a sweaty mess. I returned the car to Avis with one bar of electricity left (probably only got half of the promised mileage out of it). They gave me a lift back to my Airbnb.

What a "fun" little one-time experience! And a unique way to explore Bora Bora!

Creative Mailboxes: A Quirky Sight in Bora Bora

You see some strange things when you travel! I circled the island of Bora Bora by bike one day and by electric fun car the next. Both days, I saw about six small microwaves on posts in front of houses and near the street. Some of the microwaves were even painted. That's strange!

On some of the previous islands I visited, people got their daily bread deliveries the same way they got their mail. The mailboxes were long and skinny and open on both ends. I thought maybe someone (possibly a germaphobe) decided an enclosed container would be better for storing the bread and keeping the insects off of it.

I thought I had the riddle solved, but my curiosity wanted confirmation. I showed a photo I took of one microwave and asked a shopkeeper if that's how they got their bread deliveries. After a short pause and a small laugh, the shopkeeper said, "No, it's just a mailbox."

What a great idea for recycling a broken appliance!

The Heart of Humanity: 95% vs. 5%

I've said this many times and still believe it to be true: "95% of the people on this planet are basically good people."

Yes, there's the 5% that make the news, do mean things to you, and set wrong stereotypes for the rest of their religion, race, profession, or gender. We've all met them and could each print out a long list. BUT let's remember the 95% we've met along our way. So far on this trip, human kindness was abundant and overshadowed the rest! As I near the end of my trip, I'm being reflective and appreciating these moments of kindness. I remember:

- The friends I met on my excursions.
- Bus drivers calling out when it was my stop.
- People kindly giving me directions.
- My Mauritius fishing guide, Vimal, inviting me to his house for dinner with his wife and toddler so we could eat the fish we caught.
- People offering me a ride from the fruit stand when I realized it was a very long walk to my destination.
- My Airbnb host, Andrea, giving me a lift into town several times in the Seychelles.
- A stranger performing CPR on a drowning victim at the beach.
- Grateful strangers when I returned a found snorkel.
- Owners of the brand-new pickleball complex, Pipinya, gathering players so I could play pickleball in Sri Lanka.
- Being welcomed into the Sri Lankan home of my Florida friend, Ru, for dinner.

- People putting food and water out for the "street dogs and cats."
- The hotel manager, Ameen, in the Maldives teaching me how to fish old-school style, then cooking it for my dinner.
- The genuine kindness of the Planktons Beach Hotel staff in the Maldives.
- A local fisherman, Rafiya, teaching me how to dig sand fleas for fishing and giving me some gorgeous large shells he found while snorkeling for octopus in the Maldives.
- Being treated like a queen on Sal's farm in the Philippines.
- A traveling Facebook friend, Scott, taking the time to meet up with me for coffee and to trade travel tips.
- The friendship of Maria during my stay in Taiwan.
- Facebook friends giving support, love, and suggestions throughout my journey.
- Strangers pitching in to pull us out of the mud when we got stuck on safari.
- Local people encouraging me to try new things, no matter what they were.
- Getting help from a local in reading the French bus schedule, then later meeting up for dinner.
- Newfound friends in Tonga touring together and splitting expenses.

- Talking to friends and family by Facebook Messenger or WhatsApp on a regular basis to feel connected to home.

- The friendship of a New Zealand couple in the Cook Islands when we went to lunch together and later played cards in the lobby.

- The ukulele band playing happy birthday and the restaurant staff bringing a chocolate dessert to my table for my 60th birthday in Tahiti.

- Spending a fun day together with my friends, Dione and Robert, at their luxurious Intercontinental Resort in Tahiti.

- Kayaking every day while looking for turtles, rays, and sharks with my friendly neighbor, Ben, in Moorea.

- Getting gifts of fruit, banana bread, and coconut bread from my various neighbors and Airbnb hosts.

- All the friendly people who gave me a ride while I was hitchhiking through Huahine.

- Getting a ride to the ferry at 3:00 am from my kindhearted Airbnb hosts, Guillaume and Purotu.

- The kindness of my Airbnb hosts, Stanley and Desiree, when I brought home a Hungarian couple with broken bikes.

- Getting to go fishing with my Airbnb host, Stanley, in his boat, then eating a delicious freshly prepared fish dinner.

- The outgoing nature of French Polynesian guides in giving me a hand up, checking on me, or pulling me along when the current was too strong during a snorkel excursion. I know they get paid to do that, but there was just that little extra bit of human kindness present that makes you feel safe.

Yes, I'm sticking with my 95% vs. 5% opinion!

Broken Bikes, Attack Dogs, and Acts of Kindness

I rode my bike to the beach one day, and when I was almost home, I saw a lady going in the opposite direction topple off her bike as she was stopping to wait for her husband. Oh! I stopped and asked if she was okay. She said, "Yes, yes, no problem." I noted that she had white bandages wrapped around both of her legs below the knees. I rode on a bit and found her husband standing next to his bike, pushing on the tire. I asked if he was okay. In a heavily accented response, he said, "Defective." I crossed the road to see what was going on. He had a flat tire. I motioned and spoke slowly, asking both of them to follow me to my home Airbnb.

As soon as the three of us came into the yard, my French-speaking hostess, Desiree, came out to help. She got her English-speaking husband, Stanley, to assist as well. The couple was from Hungary and staying at a resort near the beach where I had just come from. Between all of us fumbling with language barriers, the problem was solved. Stanley put air in the tire, but it needed more than air. He also called the resort for someone to send a pickup to come and

266

get their guests and bikes. Desiree brought out a plate of chilled pamplemousse. In the meantime, all five of us sat on the shady porch and chatted in broken English. I asked what happened to the woman's bandaged legs.

The previous day, the couple had encountered a pack of seven dogs near an old, abandoned resort. Normally, there was no need to worry because the island is full of wandering dogs that mean no harm. BUT these dogs attacked! They started biting her legs! Her husband threw himself in front of her and started kicking like crazy to scare them away. She had to go to the small local clinic for her multiple wounds and to get "a shot." I assumed it was for rabies. When English is limited, there's a lot of filling in the blanks on your own. She showed me her bandages, and I could see where blood was seeping through the gauze. I couldn't imagine the terror they both experienced! I asked if she needed stitches. No, there were just a lot of puncture wounds.

As she described the pack of seven dogs, I clearly remembered encountering a pack of around seven dogs on my bike ride around the island a few days earlier. They were trotting together on my side of the road toward me while I was slowly riding along. I thought to myself, as I was all alone on that stretch of road, "Man, I hope these dogs are friendly!" They didn't do anything but continue on their way. I didn't know then just how lucky I was.

Anyway, we got the Hungarian couple all situated with their bikes in a truck and them in the cab with the driver. Hugs were given to all. I almost cried when the husband took my hand, squeezed it, and kissed it. There was a whole lot of human goodness going on for everyone that day, no matter what languages we spoke.

Fishing Adventures in Bora Bora

As you know, I love to fish and seize every opportunity to do so. When I arrived at my Airbnb bungalow in Bora Bora, my host asked if he could help arrange any excursions. I mentioned fishing, and his eyes lit up. "I like to fish, and I have a little boat," he said enthusiastically. My excitement grew!

My host, Stanley, checked the weather and suggested that 3:00 on Wednesday looked promising. I couldn't wait. The boat was moored just steps away in the lagoon behind his property. We loaded three rods and reels, the tackle box, and a cooler for our catch. And off we went.

First, we motored to a spot in the lagoon about ten meters deep. We dropped our heavily weighted lines with five feathered hooks straight down and jigged for five minutes before moving on. Each time we caught a fish, we stayed a bit longer. We moved around frequently, catching many strange-looking, colorful fish. The small ones were released, and the four keepers went into the cooler.

Once, my line suddenly jerked and then felt lighter. I reeled it in to find three hooks and the sinker missing from a cut line. Stanley explained it was a barracuda and suggested we relocate as they often travel in groups and cut fishing lines.

Another time, Stanley's rod bent sharply, and I asked if he had a big fish on the line. Calmly, he replied, "I've caught Bora Bora." I couldn't help bursting out laughing!

We wrapped up the night with four fish and plenty of fun. Desiree and Stanley prepared my jack fish for dinner—couldn't get any fresher than that!

The next evening, we decided to fish again. This time, both our lines started zinging with jacks! It was thrilling to have both lines engaged simultaneously. No barracuda incidents or catching "Bora Bora" this time, but we managed to reel in seven jacks and four other fish for a satisfying day of fishing. And we didn't even have to venture far into the lagoon to find them.

On my final night in Bora Bora, we headed out for one last fishing trip. By now, with three outings under our belts, we had a routine. We both caught fish and exchanged fishing jokes. I remarked to Stanley how fortunate he was to be able to do this every night if he wished. Indeed.

Thanks for the three memorable fishing excursions!

Swimming Among So Many Sharks

I've had the pleasure of swimming with turtles, rays, and sharks on many islands during this adventure. So why, you ask, would I want to do it again in Bora Bora?

Here's why: this shark excursion was even more exciting than previous ones due to the sheer numbers of sharks and how close they came.

I booked a Lagoon Tour that included a traditional local picnic lunch and snorkeling with stingrays and sharks. We stopped to snorkel three times, two of which included swimming with blacktip sharks.

The first stop was in deeper water outside the reef. The water was a deep blue and so clear that we could see the bottom. We were the only boat there. About 25 blacktip sharks were swimming near us but kept a cautious distance. It felt like a natural, wild experience and was amazing!

The second shark spot was the tourist hotspot where all the boats brought their guests. This spot was only three feet deep, so I didn't need a life jacket, just water shoes. It was crowded! But the stingrays and sharks didn't mind, so neither did I. It almost felt like we were a human obstacle course for them to swim around our legs!

I loved this spot even more because I could snorkel eye-to-eye with a shark! We were asked not to touch the sharks, and I was fine with that. I estimate there were between 20 to 25 blacktip sharks swimming among us during our time there. I didn't want to leave!

I absolutely loved this snorkeling excursion in Bora Bora! Want to know how much? I took 450 underwater photos of sharks and rays! The hard part was deleting 430 of them to choose the best shots. It was a fun, fun, fun day!

Lagoon Encounters: Kissed By a Stingray

As part of the full-day lagoon excursion, which also included the amazing shark experience, our group stopped at a spot teeming with stingrays, butterflyfish, and tourists. The water was only one meter deep and crystal clear. No need for a life jacket here, but water shoes provided nice protection against the broken coral bottom. I donned my snorkel mask and hopped into the turquoise water. Wow, it was like being inside an oversized aquarium! The colors of the yellow, black, and white butterflyfish were so vibrant in the clear turquoise water! The guides were dropping pieces of French baguette into the water so we could swim through the cloud of yellow. Awesome pictures!

The stingrays were also very hungry. I was unsure if they were eating the bread or if the guides were slipping fish to them. I loved watching them flap their ray wings all around the well-loved guides, their broad wings breaking the surface as they cuddled close, their bodies occasionally lifting partly out of the water in excitement. I commented, "Aw, you're getting stingray kisses! Do you think they'll do it for me?" Of course.

I took my snorkel mask off my face and placed it on top of my head. I stood up in the water next to my guide. He took the flapping, joyful stingray wings and gently transferred his buddy into my arms. We did this several times because his stingrays only had eyes for him! Eventually, they stayed long enough with me for a great close-up view, some gentle petting, and priceless photos! I've touched 100 stingrays in the past 5 months, and I always marvel at how velvety soft and smooth they feel. They are not at all slimy, as some might think. But I have to tell you, getting a hug and a kiss from a stingray takes it to a whole new level of closeness with these gorgeously strange-looking creatures.

What a treat that was!

Beeboo

Many of the Airbnb apartments or bungalows I've booked have the owners living on-site. A lot of these owners have dogs and/or cats that roam freely among the accommodations. Being a dog and cat person, this works great for me! I always ask if I'm allowed to give their pets treats or if they're allowed indoors, etc.

My favorite pet has been little Beeboo in Bora Bora. He's a small, white, soft bundle of pure puppy energy. At two years old, he still chews and runs like a puppy.

Beeboo would always come to greet me when I got home from an excursion or when I went to the main house for any reason. He would sneak over to my bungalow and sit and cuddle with me while I read my Kindle on the patio. He also let me know when he wanted to play by chewing on my newly fixed Vionic sandals while they were on my feet! No, Beeboo!

One day, he was in the yard chewing on one of my old pizza crusts that had been dug out of the trashcan by a stray cat. I picked it up and threw it, and by golly, figured out he liked to play fetch! We did that until we were both tired!

Beeboo would also run and jump into the boat when we went fishing. He wanted to go everywhere. "Not this time, Beeboo," my Airbnb host would say.

Beeboo also had a naughty streak. Not only did he bite and chew, but he also jumped. Those little claws wreaked havoc on my 60-year-old arms with thin skin. You'd have thought I was in a fight and lost with all the dark red marks on my forearms!

Despite his naughtiness, he was an adorable little fluffball accessory to my bungalow for the week. I will really miss hearing, "Beeboo, NO!"

Relaxing Sunset Dinner at the Yacht Club

In my search for unique activities that aren't repeated from island to island (no need to feel sorry for me for enjoying too much paradise), I discovered that a sunset dinner at the Yacht Club was a possibility. My host, Desiree, made the reservation for me. Most of the local upscale restaurants offer hotel pickup and return. This was perfect because I had no desire to ride my bicycle to dinner in a dress!

Yes, I put on the one and only dress I had packed. I clipped a fake flower behind my right ear, donned my gold bracelet and the gold earrings that replaced those that were "pinched" in Tonga, and stood next to the road outside my Airbnb. I was super excited for a nice dinner and sunset.

I stood by the road 15 minutes early because I'd rather be early than one minute late. Nobody came. Fifteen minutes later, still nobody came. Where the heck was my free transportation? I began to sweat after 30 minutes in the sun, standing beside the road (waste of a perfectly good shower).

My host came out to let me know that she had scheduled the reservation for 5:30, not 5:00. Our limited English/French communication had me thinking I'd miss the sunset, which was the whole point of paying for an expensive sunset dinner.

Finally, the taxi came, and I made it to the Yacht Club right at 5:30. I ordered a happy hour drink and snapped photos for 10 minutes straight as the sun disappeared at 5:40. My table was right at the edge of the dock with an unobstructed view! There were a dozen sailboats anchored, and little dinghies brought diners over from those boats or the neighboring motus. How beautiful! This was one of those times on my trip when I wished for a companion to share this stunning view.

After the sun disappeared, I focused on the menu. I usually start with dessert because life is too short—eat dessert first! This way, I get the good stuff first and can always take home half of my dinner for lunch the next day. I ordered the crème brûlée, and it was fabulous!

Next, I ordered scallops and mashed potatoes. I love scallops and have rarely met one I didn't like. These were pretty but had no flavor. I added salt but just couldn't reach THAT taste I was looking for. But that's okay because the crème brûlée made up for it!

While enjoying my meal and the view, I overheard a nearby American accent. When the young couple came by my table to take sunset photos, we struck up a conversation. They were from Colorado and Florida (both my stomping grounds) and were honeymooning in French Polynesia. We chatted for a while and exchanged Instagram info.

As I was waiting to pay my bill, I stood next to the lit dock in front of my table and watched as fish and a shark cruised by. What a relaxed, upscale, beautiful evening at the Yacht Club.

Rough Rides and Rich Stories: A 4x4 Safari in Bora Bora

On my last day in Bora Bora, I joined the half-day 4x4 Safari tour of the island. Having already explored the perimeter, I knew this was the only way to see the middle!

The 4x4 pickup, with bench seats and guard rails in the back, rolled up to the gate of my Airbnb at 8:15 am. There was another couple in the back, so the driver told me to sit in the front with him. Better view and not as rough a ride. Maybe.

We bumped and rattled our way to some very interesting sites! We saw the place where human sacrifices were once made. We saw one of the 100 American bunkers left from WWII. I met Flore, a granddaughter of a G.I. We were shown the only spot on the barrier reef where ships can pass through into the lagoon from the Pacific Ocean. (This path was created with dynamite by United States soldiers during WWII.) Our guide also pointed out the airport on the nearby Motu Mute. We visited several sacred sites and looked out over the lagoon from some fascinating viewing stops.

Because our guide was such a comedian, it was sometimes hard to tell when he was joking or telling us facts. One such story was about the use of pigs as a GPS. Originally, no land animals were on Bora Bora, but dogs, chickens, and pigs were brought over. When captains needed to find land, they would throw some of their pigs into the water. Because pigs swim toward the nearest body of land, they used the pigs' instinct as their GPS. I'm not sure if he was pulling a fast one on us, but it seemed just crazy enough to be true. You decide.

Also, when James Cook came to Bora Bora, he picked up navigator Tupaia to accompany him. Tupaia spoke clear English and was the translator between Cook and the natives. The question here is, if James Cook was supposedly the first explorer to land on Bora Bora, where did Tupaia learn to be so fluent in English? Hmmm…

All in all, it was a great tour filled with stories of magic, facts, a little BS, and a half-day of bumpy fun!

Is It Really Over?

My trip is almost over, and it's time to start making my way back home. There are no international flights out of Bora Bora, only from Tahiti. I wanted to be in Papeete early to catch my flight from Tahiti to Los Angeles without any delays. To ensure this, I booked my flight from Bora Bora back to Papeete, allowing myself one night in Tahiti just in case something went wrong.

You may remember that the airport in Bora Bora is not on the mainland. It's on Motu Mute, which is a 15-minute ferry ride from the mainland. The price of the ferry is included in the cost of the airline ticket.

My Airbnb host generously gave me a ride to the ferry, and we waved goodbye. I waited on a bench for my Air Moana ferry to arrive, but I was in the wrong line for 10 minutes before I discovered my mistake. I was getting nervous because the ferry schedule and flight schedule were only one hour apart. I talked to someone else in line, and she reassured me there was only one flight on this airline, and we were all on it. Okie dokie, island time…

The ferry arrived, we all boarded with our suitcases, and we were treated to a farewell sunset! Wow, that's going out with a bang!

The airport check-in went smoothly, and there was no security check, so I was able to keep my bottle of water. YES! Oh, the little things.

After landing in Papeete, I spent all my leftover CFP francs on an after-hours taxi and made it to my less-than-stellar hotel with an ugly view, spotty Wi-Fi, and limited hot water. I think it's a good thing that I can leave paradise (Bora Bora) with fond memories, and my "layover" in Papeete is gross so I'll be excited to get home instead of wishing I could stay in Tahiti.

Making lemonade out of lemons…

Home, Sweet Home

After a flight from my final island of Bora Bora, followed by an overnight flight from Papeete to Los Angeles, I re-checked my tiny suitcase for my next two flights to get me back to my home in Florida.

Wow, 38 flights, 28 different accommodations, five months, and a bucket load of amazing experiences!

I got a tear in my eye when I went through customs at LAX and saw the giant sign with a United States flag that read, "Welcome to the United States of America." I also felt a sense of gratitude when I walked back into my own home. My renters had left it in immaculate condition! I took a 20-minute shower with a consistent flow of hot water. My air conditioner was running. I threw a load of laundry into the washing machine AND dryer! I drove my car to the store to buy groceries and was happy to be able to read the labels.

I played pickleball and met up with friends. I went bass fishing.

I love traveling, exploring, and meeting amazing people. This "Island Buffet" was an experience that only comes once in a lifetime. There were so many invaluable lessons learned on this solo journey.

No matter how much fun I had, I must admit, there's no place like home!

Travel Takeaways: One Word for Each Island

Here's a one-word description of my takeaway from each island:

- Mauritius – Friendly
- Réunion – Upscale
- Madagascar – Poor
- Seychelles – Picturesque
- Sri Lanka – Happy
- Maldives – Amazing
- Philippines – Delicious
- Taiwan – Efficient
- Papua New Guinea – Untamed
- Vanuatu – Rainy

- New Caledonia – French
- Tonga – Proud
- Cook Islands – Giving
- Tahiti – Touristy
- Moorea – Active
- Huahine – Slow
- Bora Bora – Genuine
- This wonderful opportunity – Priceless

My top five, in no particular order, are the Maldives, the Philippines, the Cook Islands, Moorea, and Bora Bora.

For those planning upcoming trips, here are some suggestions based on my top five:

- Trip 1: Cook Islands, Moorea, and Bora Bora
- Trip 2: Philippines
- Trip 3: Maldives and Seychelles

Thanks for joining me in this amazing adventure. Happy travels!

- Wikipedia Contributors. "Mauritius." Wikipedia, The Free Encyclopedia. Wikipedia, The Free Encyclopedia, 1 January 2024. *Web. https://en.wikipedia.org/wiki/Mauritius.*

- Wikipedia Contributors. "Réunion." Wikipedia, The Free Encyclopedia. Wikipedia, The Free Encyclopedia, 8 January 2024. *Web. https://en.wikipedia.org/wiki/Réunion.*

- Wikipedia Contributors. "Madagascar." Wikipedia, The Free Encyclopedia. Wikipedia, The Free Encyclopedia, 22 January 2024. *Web. https://en.wikipedia.org/wiki/Madagascar.*

- Wikipedia Contributors. "Seychelles." Wikipedia, The Free Encyclopedia. Wikipedia, The Free Encyclopedia, 31 January 2024. *Web. https://en.wikipedia.org/wiki/Seychelles.*

- Wikipedia Contributors. "Sri Lanka." Wikipedia, The Free Encyclopedia. Wikipedia, The Free Encyclopedia, 10 February 2024. *Web. https://en.wikipedia.org/wiki/Sri_Lanka.*

- Wikipedia Contributors. "Maldives." Wikipedia, The Free Encyclopedia. Wikipedia, The Free Encyclopedia, 20 February 2024. *Web. https://en.wikipedia.org/wiki/Maldives.*

- Wikipedia Contributors. "Philippines." Wikipedia, The Free Encyclopedia. Wikipedia, The Free Encyclopedia, 28 February 2024. *Web. https://en.wikipedia.org/wiki/Philippines.*

- Wikipedia Contributors. "Taiwan." Wikipedia, The Free Encyclopedia. Wikipedia, The Free Encyclopedia, 7 March 2024. *Web. https://en.wikipedia.org/wiki/Taiwan.*

- Wikipedia Contributors. "Papua New Guinea." Wikipedia, The Free Encyclopedia. Wikipedia, The Free Encyclopedia, 15 March 2024. *Web. https://en.wikipedia.org/wiki/Papua_New_Guinea.*

- Wikipedia Contributors. "Vanuatu." Wikipedia, The Free Encyclopedia. Wikipedia, The Free Encyclopedia, 22 March 2024. *Web. https://en.wikipedia.org/wiki/Vanuatu.*

- Wikipedia Contributors. "New Caledonia." Wikipedia, The Free Encyclopedia. Wikipedia, The Free Encyclopedia, 30 March 2024. *Web. https://en.wikipedia.org/wiki/New_Caledonia.*

- Wikipedia Contributors. "Tonga." Wikipedia, The Free Encyclopedia. Wikipedia, The Free Encyclopedia, 6 April 2024. *Web. https://en.wikipedia.org/wiki/Tonga.*

- Wikipedia Contributors. "Cook Islands." Wikipedia, The Free Encyclopedia. Wikipedia, The Free Encyclopedia, 13 April 2024. *Web. https://en.wikipedia.org/wiki/Cook_Islands.*

- Wikipedia Contributors. "Tahiti." Wikipedia, The Free Encyclopedia. Wikipedia, The Free Encyclopedia, 20 April 2024. *Web. https://en.wikipedia.org/wiki/Tahiti.*

- Wikipedia Contributors. "Moorea." Wikipedia, The Free Encyclopedia. Wikipedia, The Free Encyclopedia, 27 April 2024. *Web. https://en.wikipedia.org/wiki/Moorea.*

- Wikipedia Contributors. "Huahine." Wikipedia, The Free Encyclopedia. Wikipedia, The Free Encyclopedia, 4 May 2024. *Web. https://en.wikipedia.org/wiki/Huahine.*

- Wikipedia Contributors. "Bora Bora." Wikipedia, The Free Encyclopedia. Wikipedia, The Free Encyclopedia, 12 May 2024. *Web. https://en.wikipedia.org/wiki/Bora_Bora.*